Change YOUR MIND Change YOUR MONEY

LATOYA MADDOX

Change YOUR MIND Change YOUR MONEY

Published by Krystal Lee Enterprises (KLE Publishing) Please send comments and questions:

Krystal Lee Enterprises
770-240-0089 Ext. 1
sales@KLEPub.com

To Reach the Author:
Phone: 678-971-3861
Address: 5051 Peachtree Corners Circle Suite 200
Norcross, GA 30092
Web: infinitywealthadvisors.net
Facebook: facebook.com/infinityfinancialllc
Linkedin: linkedin.com/in/latoyamaddox/

Printed in the United States of America.

ISBN: 979-8-89987-945-6

Dedication & Acknowledgments

To the cycle breakers.
To the wealth builders.
To the ones who refuse to let money control their future.
This book is dedicated to you —
The person ready to change your thinking so you can change your outcomes.
Your financial security is not an accident.
It is a decision.

- LaToya

Writing a book about financial empowerment is deeply personal. It requires honesty, vulnerability, and a willingness to challenge long-held beliefs. I am deeply grateful to the people who supported me through every draft, revision, and late-night burst of inspiration.

To my family and friends — thank you for your patience, encouragement, and belief in my mission. Your support gave me the space and confidence to create.

To my clients — you are my daily inspiration. Your questions, courage, and commitment to growth shaped the insights shared in these pages. It is an honor to walk alongside you as you build clarity and confidence around your money.

To the mentors, colleagues, and industry leaders who sharpened my thinking and strengthened my practice — your wisdom has influenced this work more than you know.

To the women navigating transition — divorce, retirement, reinvention — you remind me that financial security is not just about numbers. It is about confidence, clarity, and control.

To my mother — though our path together was complicated at times, I am grateful for the healing, understanding, and love we found before your passing. Through life's challenges, I learned resilience, compassion, forgiveness, and the power of perseverance. Your story is forever woven into mine, and your memory continues to inspire me. I am grateful that we found our way back to one another and were able to grow closer in the years we shared together.

To my grandmother — thank you for your unwavering love, wisdom, and strength. Your presence in my life is a daily reminder that faith, family, and perseverance can carry us through any season. I am grateful for the lessons you have taught me and for the legacy of resilience that continues through our family.

To my husband, **Donald** — thank you for supporting all of my "crazy ideas." Thank you for listening to business strategies at the dinner table, for encouraging the vision before it was fully formed, and for believing in me even when I questioned myself. Your steady presence, humor, and quiet strength make it possible for me to dream boldly and execute courageously. I could not do this without you.

And to our children — **Joseph, Joshua, and Logan** — everything I build is with your future in mind. I want you to see what discipline looks like. What faith looks like. What ownership looks like. I live and lead by example so that you will never shrink your dreams, question your worth, or doubt your ability to create opportunity.

Logan, my future trailblazer — Mommy wants the world for you. May you always know that you are capable, called, and equipped to build your own legacy.

Finally, to every reader — thank you for choosing to invest your time in yourself. May this book serve as both a mirror and a roadmap. May it challenge you, empower you, and remind you that financial security begins in the mind.

Change YOUR MIND Change YOUR MONEY

TABLE OF CONTENTS

Introduction

Money is a sensitive subject for most people, but for women who are running their households, it is downright uncomfortable more often than not. We do not enjoy having to think of "robbing Peter to pay Paul" scenarios to make it through the week. Living paycheck to paycheck can be a strain, the same as going from doing well to all of a sudden financial turmoil. The life of a woman is dynamic and multi-dimensional, and my life and circumstances are no different.

I wrote this book because I know how hard it can be to rebuild your life when the initial foundation was never secure. When you look over your shoulder or reflect on your life, the most vivid pictures are broken homes, marriages, disappointments, and financial strain. The last thing you want to do is spend more time thinking about something you feel you cannot change, financial worries.

Some of us have been broke or struggling for so long that it has become our new normal. Oftentimes we fall into the trap of thinking more money means more problems. I want to interrupt your mindset and present to you another perspective of how your life can be. If you are recently divorced and the life you have built is in shambles, allow me to point you to a way of escape. If you are overwhelmed by debt, dealing with bad credit (By the way, there is no such thing as bad credit; I call it challenged credit. More on that later.), and can't buy or rent a place to save your life. I can throw you a lifeline. If you have never had an understanding of financial literacy and you believe it is too much or too soon to think about your financial future, I am here to tell you to think again.

Challenges and setbacks happen to us all. We don't know when a person will leave this earth or when our financial picture or health will take a turn. The secret sauce to life, and what I found separates the haves from the have-nots, or those who tend to be comfortable during a storm, is preparation. Yes, we cannot control everything that happens in our lives, but in the areas you can control, I want to show you how to have authority over them.

Journey through my story and others that I have helped to turn their lives around by zeroing in on their money game. To change your financial picture is to change your life's outcome. So let's do the good work of Changing Your Mind so that we can Change Your Money.

Chapter 1

Are You Like Me?

Before you think too deeply about the contents of this book, I want to calm your fears. This book is not going to be dominated by charts, numbers, or mental strength exercises. This book is not my autobiography or a chain of unrelatable and impractical pieces of advice that skip over your pain points. This book will touch on matters of your heart, issues you are facing today, and prove to be one of the most impactful guides you will find. Not only because of the information, but its ability to be implemented in practical ways that will show instant results in your life.

So, what are some of the challenges or problems with your finances today? Do you have enough money to live comfortably? Do you feel comfortable with how much you have put away for a rainy day because those days always come? How about retirement? Have you saved or invested enough to know that your children and spouse will be okay? What is your vision for you and their financial futures?

Or are you like many who have not taken a deep look at their finances? Like the ones who have some money saved, but if you are honest, you could have had more. You have little to no money invested, although you know you should. You may have an insurance policy, but it has been years since you looked at it. We kind of throw things into a junk drawer, knowing someday we will need it. But do you know how putting off these decisions is impacting your life?

Have you considered what your life could be like today if you found a way to marry your future plans with your current demands? Life has a way of guiding us even if we think to go with the flow. That flow can mean us falling down a waterfall of challenges into an unknown body of water beneath. Some of us can land in peaceable waters, while others end up in a current where we can barely come up for air. We are tossed wherever our finances take us, and we are more reactionary than proactive.

It is easy to fall into this trap, and it is why so many people take the risk. Yes, you cannot avoid everything, but a lot can be avoided. You can be smart about your money, but that only happens when you are knowledgeable about your challenges, disadvantages, and opportunities. You may have heard the saying "Money can buy anything except love and respect."

However, to be in a relationship, marriage, caring for children, and hanging out with friends all cost money and equally time. Let's be honest, most of us struggle with our time and money. How you manage your time is also linked to how you spend your money. The time you are spending right now to get your money in alignment with your plans, dreams, and vision for the future is not only a good use of time, but it will impact your money.

Now that I have your attention, my name is LaToya Maddox, and I am a Certified Financial Planner. I help my clients in the areas of insurance, retirement planning, and investing. I have not always operated with a financially educated mindset when managing my own finances. Like you, I was living life and allowing my money to do what I thought it needed to do to keep me safe. I will get into more of this in a minute. The point is, I wasn't born with a silver spoon in my mouth, nor did I come from a traditional home.

My mother and grandmother raised me, along with a few key women in my life who supported me throughout my youth and early adult life. I didn't have the best relationship with my mom while growing up. I know when we watch movies and see baked cookies, happy smiles, and this feminine love in the air between mother and daughter–I didn't have that. My mom was a very vocal woman who was equally headstrong. She blurted out her opinions and tended to live life on her terms. I appreciated her like any good daughter should.

No woman is perfect, nor is it possible to get it all right. I wanted to be closer to my mom, like any child, but that too, wasn't always the case. My mom was a person that made a lot of decisions on a whim. Her emotions and views on things seemed to take precedence over anything else. Her decisions, likewise, were not thought out in the sense of how they would impact us financially. If she got mad with someone or on the job, it would be enough for her to walk out.

Unfortunately, the same approach she had with picking up and leaving jobs she took to where we lived. My mother would have a bad encounter with someone, the neighbor, the landlord, or a friend, and she would pack up and leave. Not all of these moves were close to where we were before, either. I remember relocating to entirely different areas altogether plenty of times, and it was challenging.

I never spent more than two years at any given school. It just didn't feel right. Just when I would get comfortable somewhere, my scenery would change. Growing up, I went to at least 9 different schools - there are only 12 years of school, counting elementary and high school. I used to be able to name them all, and if I sat down to think hard enough, I could name most of them. So, long-term friends were never part of my picture. I would also argue building a strong interest or connection with teachers and my community wasn't developed. I had a get-up-and-go mentality because that was my environment.

It was either me and my grandmother or my mom and I when she wasn't spending time sleeping off a hangover. Yes, my mom was an alcoholic, and I didn't lead with that because alcoholism was a cover-up of her heart's true emotions about life. Later, I actually discovered she suffered from Bipolar Disorder. This explained a lot of her erratic decision-making.

Sometimes, we are in various situations not because of our choices but because of our environment. Consider what connections you have formed with money based on your environment. What takes on life have you developed because this is what your parents believed? How have other people's choices impacted your life and living conditions?

I remember when I was about to start my senior year of high school, I received some bad news. I was not allowed to register because my grandmother had moved out of the district. Unlike how today, you can apply to attend a school out of your district, we couldn't do that growing up. Or, they were being so tight about the rules they didn't care how their choices impacted my life. It may sound easy and be the right thing to do, just to go to the new school, right?

Only, I couldn't. At this point, for me, the pot had finally boiled over. Years of moving annually and the impact of not having roots anywhere long enough to build anything was bothering me greatly. If I switched and attended the new school, that would have been the third school I attended since enrolling in high school! Can you imagine the pressure to start each year practically being the new girl, how that felt for me?

I was never comfortable and seemed to never fit in. I wanted one year to go to the same school for 2 consecutive years where it mattered. Your junior and senior years mattered not only for high school but for college. My hopes for attending college were shaky, but graduating from college was proven even more challenging with my moving history, classes, and credits.

There are only 4 yrs of high school, and I saw no point in being the new girl or student at someone's school my senior year. This was the year I should have enjoyed myself the most with prom, events, and hanging out with friends before they went to college. However, because I constantly moved and was never in one school for long, I would have missed out on all of that.

To make things worse, I never took part in any clubs or extracurricular activities. I didn't want to be the girl that played on both sides. One year with my friends, and the next a rival school where I was versus the friends I had just made. It also seemed counterproductive. My senior year, I just knew that this year mattered more than the others. My senior year was the last year I had to normalize my high school years; and between school administrations and life circumstances, it didn't look like it would come together.

This was one of my life's early tests of grit. My high school principal, Mr. Elrod (who happened to be my 4th-grade gym teacher in another school district), understood my plight and said to come to school on the first day, and he would admit me. Yay, I thought my prayers had been answered, and my fear was assuaged. Fast forward to the first day of school, now. I arrived and found out that Mr. Elrod's father had passed away and that he was out for the week. My guidance counselor, Ms. Larson, stepped in and promptly told me I had no choice but to go to Rich South. She gave me my transcripts and sent me on my way.

I arrived at Rich South and met my new guidance counselor. She looked over my transcripts and rudely began to tell me what classes they were not going to be able to take. I was an honor student with stellar grades. I honestly didn't know what she was talking about. I didn't trust her tone and the way she was treating me. I took my transcripts out of her hand and sharply told her she didn't have to worry about me because I was not coming to this school.

In hindsight, that took guts. I had no plan or idea what to do next. All I knew was I didn't like the way my new school/guidance counselor was treating me. I promptly went home and started thinking of a plan:

Option #1: pay out-of-district tuition.
Option #2: get my GED
Option #3: wait for Mr. Elrod to return

I called my mother and she had a fit. She immediately said, "You are dropping out of school to be with your boyfriend, ain't you? LaToya, you are too smart for this. This, right here, is not smart at all. And what you need to do is take your butt back to that school and do what they say."

I told her my other options because going back, I wasn't doing. She quickly advised me, "I am not paying for anything. You make this decision, you are on your own." I couldn't afford to pay for tuition, and I really didn't want to get a GED. Since options one and two were gone, I had to go with three. So, I decided to wait for Mr. Elrod to come back.

Two weeks later, I would be enrolled in junior college for 3 courses, a correspondence psychology class, and night school gym. This was the prescription given to me in order to complete my senior year. I quickly got a job working at Syberis to pay for it all. When I look back, I am amazed at my actions. I knew not to tolerate anything less than respectful treatment, so I decided to take my own life into my own hands.

My independence was solidified while I was in my senior year of high school. No, it was not because of a relationship, a baby, or anything that people may stereotype for alternative education. I performed well, I did what I was supposed to do, and yet, I was slighted from having the experience everyone thinks is normal. That was when I realized I could do anything and that I was responsible for how my life turned out.

Although I had a mother, I could not rely on her to ensure what I wanted for me happened. Bless my grandmother, but she, too, had bills and a life she had to live. With that, I charted a course that I stuck to to graduate and take care of myself. I was able to graduate from Crete-Monee with my class. I missed out on major senior moments like prom, senior days, and other trips. It was a hard year to see what I lost and missed out on. I know personally what it felt like to be kicked out of school for being pregnant for those who have that story and had to attend night school.

Although I got the paper diploma, I did not get to walk across the stage. My senior year was like my other years in a sense, however, this time, I felt it was on my terms. I did feel some of my power coming and being magnified by what I was able to accomplish for myself. At the time, I was okay with it.

I picked up my diploma and drove it to my mother's house because I was living with my grandma at the time. I remember saying to her as I held up my diploma, "You thought I was going to be a dropout." She smiled and took my diploma to read it more intently. It made me smile more because I knew what it took for me to get it. She knew what it took for her to help me in the ways she could.

My mom couldn't give me everything I wanted, but she and my grandmother did give me what I needed. I am grateful for those who stepped up in my life because they helped build my confidence. I would never have made that decision when I was in high school had someone done it for me. In their absence, I started the foundation that landed me a career job while in high school. While others were pursuing senior activities, I was laying the foundation for my career and business.

You see, the way you feel about yourself does matter. I thought of myself higher than the way I was treated, and I obtained my diploma. I set my sights on something I wanted, and I worked to get it. The value you put on your choices matters. What you value in life will be manifested in how you manage your finances. The same is true for how you keep your home and how you treat yourself.

The internal battles my mom faced showed up in her relationships and her relationship with money. The end result was unstable finances, housing, and a lack of emotional support that not only impacted her, but me also. Things that are so important to a child, I missed out on and swore not to allow my child to suffer in the same way. I wanted a normal life, but I had the complete opposite.

I know for many of us growing up like me, having a parent who was a heavy drinker may have been the norm. At an early age, I knew that life must be different, and I was determined to create a new normal for myself. Growing up with my mother, I learned to move quickly but take my time to get comfortable with people and situations. I may have secretly developed a phobia of not having enough money in the bank. I was scared of poverty and only felt comfortable if I saw a certain amount of money in my bank accounts. I waited as long as I did to have children, even though I was married for years because I refused to bring a child into this world and not be able to provide.

You see, my life circumstances helped to develop my relationship with money even when I thought the two had nothing to do with each other.

I want you to take a moment and ask yourself the question, what is your relationship with money like? How have you spent, saved, and used your money over the years? Do you have a strong grip on your cash, or is it loose? Do you count every penny or spend without checks and balances?

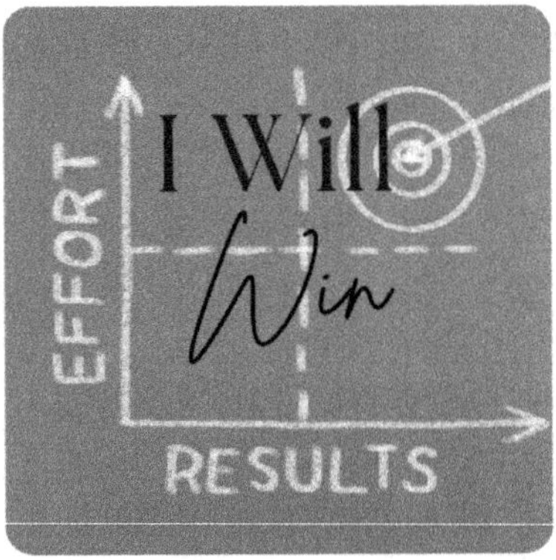

Your attitude towards money has been shaped by your experiences. You may think your experiences may have little or nothing to do with money. Or that how you grew up bears no importance for how you see money, but it does. I am here to tell you there is a direct correlation between your past experiences and how you handle money today. It wasn't until I had to address two major problems head-on early in life that I learned to reshape my relationship with money.

Chapter 2
Improving Your Circumstances

If you are still thinking of changing your relationship with money, keep reading. You are at the tip of the mountain, but with me as your guide, I can take you up the mountain. But as I told you in the previous chapter, we have to get rid of some old things to embrace the new. A good question: ***What can you purge so that you can honestly move on in life?***

I will start with a personal example of what I did to unravel my tight grip on money and concepts of how I used money. Then, I will explain how to make this nugget applicable to your life. In my case, my mother had an addiction; yes, she also suffered from a mental disorder. My mother had an issue that was affecting her, and upon examination in my later years this showed up my relationship with money.

On the one hand, I was disappointed with the life I had to live. Not having a solid foundation made me cling to what I could control. Money was a way my anxiety was manifested, but also my fear of poverty and uncertainty. Growing up with limited means can make us humble and teach an invaluable lesson of learning how to get along with less. However, it also can breed a not-enough spirit that will cause you to operate out of lack fueled by fear. Also known as the scarcity mindset.

When we are afraid of something, we tend to overcompensate in one area. If you are afraid of poverty, you may become an excessive saver or even a hoarder. You don't want to throw anything away because you may fear you will need it again. Maybe your sweet memories are locked into that item, so you think throwing the object away is associated with losing the memory. It may not make rational sense, but it is how our minds and hearts can work.

In my case, I needed to see a certain dollar amount in my bank account to ward off my fear of poverty. Then, when I saw the targeted dollar figure, I came up with other excuses for wanting to see more before I would vacation or enjoy any of the money I had made. I didn't have a proper balance with money because I didn't have a good balance in my relationships. I needed to clear the air with my past so that I could see a future that was different.

In order to move past this money block, I needed to forgive my mother and release what I thought my life should have been like and create a new vision for myself. My mom and I had a heart to heart when I graduated from Georgia State University in 2002 with my undergraduate degree. The best conversation of both of our lives and we each needed it.

Personally, I am glad I did mend things with my mom. Her habits over the years did take a toll on her health and she died at 52 years old. I cannot imagine what life could have been like for me holding a grudge or having discontentment within my heart after her death because I didn't take advantage of the time we had.

Forgiving someone and choosing to move on may feel tough in the beginning but it really frees you more than entraps you. It didn't cure her addiction, make her drink less, or fix her disease. I understood it was important for me to process my past so that I could form the new habits I had to make to change my money behaviors. I am thinking you, too, need to change some of your behaviors by addressing habits that were formed from experience.

What are some of those experiences that shape your view and relationship with money? In my practice, many people come to me to help them when they are heading to divorce or are recently divorced. It can feel like you have been punched in the gut when you wake up to an empty room and tons of bills. I have women coming into my office and they are really at their limit of what they can take. I assure them it won't be a quick fix, but we can get a game plan that will allow them to breathe.

Changing your money habits does not happen overnight. Some changes will be gradual, while others will be instantaneous. If you were used to living off a two-person household and one income is now gone, you instantly feel the brunt. It can take you time to adjust to living within your means and you tend to become more mindful–eventually. These adjustments often bring tears of anger, frustration, or disappointment.

It is okay. The first step to improving your circumstances with anything, is you have to see and understand what they are. If you have items on autopay, bills that were generated when your house was larger, or habits like cooking big meals, you may need to revise. When relationships end or take a new direction, it is an adjustment, and life is not the same as usual.

Another client I often have visiting me is those who are experiencing expansion. This could be a married couple having children, my client who is getting married, or a client who is getting a raise on the job. It might sound silly at first to need a financial planner because you got a raise. But I can tell you, most people who receive a raise, without a plan for the increase, tend to not realize the monetary impact because their money habits didn't change.

If you have a tendency to spend without a budget on less money, the same is true with a larger income. The principle and the root cause for your decision to buy is virtually the same, and that has to change if you want a different outcome.

The second step to a good financial planner's attempt to revamp your money situation is to look at places where they can find or save money. Seeing your bank accounts, bills, and spending history will say a lot about your habits and your view on money. These trends were not out of thin air, but were likely worked in by your lifestyle.

There are some key questions you should ask yourself as you start to get a handle on your finances. For example, do you have a budget? Secondly, is that budget realistic? When I created my first budget, I had a scarcity mindset. I put away every penny, and I made zero time for fun. I was building my empire, after all! I had no time for trips, dinners, outings, or anything that didn't benefit my bottom line.

But when I learned to release the pain I had from my upbringing, I wanted to be happy. It made me happy to travel, enjoy nice dinners, and buy purses every now and again. I never went crazy, but I started to find excitement in spending my money on things I loved as well as saving it. I found that balance between saving and spending without guilt. If you have never had a financial planner look at your specific situation and see how they can help you plan a future you too can love, I invite you to give me a call.

What the call will not be, is a sales pitch. One thing you will learn in business, your ideal clients are among the ones you help. If you have a mindset to help people and they want what you are offering, you will find your clients among the crowd. I have been doing this for many years, and I am in love with seeing people transform their situations. People who came to me were struggling when we met because they were saddled with debt, got full custody, or had to pay a large sum of child support.

After a few months of adjustments, we often begin to see benefits. This is why I got into financial services. Everyone I help also helps me to stay in balance. Seeing life happen reminds me to live. After our call, there are a few things you will be able to do to change your financial picture. It is hard to invest or speak about insurance policies if you don't have the money. BUT, if you have a trade, skill, or something you can teach someone, you can find the money. The subject of entrepreneurship must be spoken about.

Too often, I find we limit ourselves based on what we were told or experienced if we have tried it before. If you tried to start a business and it failed, or if you went for a promotion and got denied. These experiences can mute your self-worth and make you question your abilities. I want to encourage you that what you have now is not all that you will have. You can believe for more even if you don't see it yet. However, you have to be prepared to make some changes to your life choices.

First example, my Case Study, we will call her Michelle. She came into my office because she had a mother who always had a problem. Month-to-month, her mother would come and ask her for money. She, of course, felt bad and even felt responsible for taking care of her mother. When she would not oblige her mother's request, she would threaten her with living on the streets.

Do you have a family member that is manipulative like this? Do they threaten you with leaving or doing something half-crazy to get you to support them or their decisions financially? Unfortunately, you are not the only one.

Now, back to Michelle. She came to me, and her finances were all over the place. I told her after looking over her documents, "Good news, I am a financial planner, and I can work a miracle, but, I don't perform magic. To get your finances in order, Michelle, we are going to have to cut back on spending. And to do that, I am going to have to ask you to set some boundaries."

She had everything she needed to help herself out of this situation, but she needed to find her voice and level of importance in her life. Yes, we owe our parents a big thank you for giving us life, and we will help support them in ways we can. However, if you allow your ship to go down, then you are no longer able to help anyone else. When you are on the plane, they say to put on your own mask first, then help your children, neighbors, or others.

It is that same approach that I would tell you: To fix your finances, you must put your mask on first. You have to make a budget for yourself, and you gotta stick to it. When your mom comes, children, friends, or others, remind them what the goal is. If you are married, you likely are going to come up with this decision together. Be sure you both share the same goal of saving and budgeting. Being in agreement over money also helps to avoid arguing over money.

If you owe someone something, make it a priority to pay it back. This is a good habit with borrowing, your credit, but also with forgiveness. If you owe an apology or you received one from someone else, release the person from the debt. Some people will not be able to pay for all the pain they caused you. Sometimes you cannot pay, and fall into the same category. With our parents, we do have to learn to see them as human and let some things go.

When we let go of one thing, it frees up our hands to grab ahold of something else. To help Michelle along her journey, I had her do a money makeover challenge. During this challenge, she had to learn to commit to an action plan and implement it for at least 30 days to see the results. Her results after 30 days varied, but two things she did that I loved. She established boundaries with her mother, and she had a benevolent fund in place that allowed her to give a set amount to manage her money better.

Sometimes, it is not cutting people out of your life but planning their needs in your budget so that you both can breathe. If you feel like your circumstances have taken control over your life, you are one appliance breakdown from ruin. I want you to consider doing the 30-day Money Makeover challenge also. We can make living pay-check to pay-check normal, but that doesn't mean it should be.

Access Free Resources
Scan or Visit
latoyamaddox.com

I am sure you have heard it said that it takes 21 days to form a new habit. I agree that it takes time, but for some of us, it can take a bit longer. So 30 days is not a long time to spend on untangling choices you have been making for decades, likely. If you don't have a financial planner or will not do a consultation, commit to 30 days of shedding unnecessary spending. Looking at your finances and determining what you want out of life is so important.

It may sound simple, but if you want to vacation, you have to plan for it. You can take a vacation on any budget, and depending on how much you make and how much the trip costs may determine the time frame. But don't give up on what you would like to have because it means you have to work for it. You will appreciate that trip so much more than those who charge it and are stressing out about debt.

One thing I have to warn you about that I found out through experience. When you see that this program works and you carve out money, it may be tempting to tell people about it. I want you to tell them about the program that helped you to save money, but be careful on telling people the amount. I remember when I saved up six thousand dollars. I was so proud of myself and I had to tell someone. At this time, I told my first husband.

Do you know, once he found out I had saved up that money, everything that could need money needed it? What took months to build up took seemingly weeks or days to burn through. Out of sight, out of mind. I learned then to have multiple bank accounts that I had with money in them I didn't touch. I only checked them on occasion to prevent fraud.

But as I said, people who lack discipline with their spending will not correct with more money. They tend to spend more once they know they have access to more. So if you want to help yourself or someone else save money, keep what you save out of mind so you are not tempted to use it. I know for some of us we have been saving for a vacation for what seems like forever because whenever we get close to going, something happens.

I have to tell you that you are not God, and you cannot save everyone. If I did everything people asked of me, I would be in their position, too. Don't feel guilty as you grow in your finances for being disciplined.

Another good bonus to being balanced with your finances is good credit. Having good credit impacts everything about your life, and you should take it seriously. Don't be quick to co-sign or jump on the bandwagon because someone you loved asked for a loan. Not everyone can or will pay you back, unfortunately. Make a budget for what you will give monthly and stick to it. When it is gone, it is gone.

After completing this exercise, it will take some effort to manifest your desires–but it can be done! So, let's see how to move forward and put your desires into action. In the next chapter, Cleaning Out Your Junk Drawer, we will pull out the details you have hanging out in your all-purpose drawer.

Financial Checkup

Take a moment to assess where you are today. Answer the following questions honestly. There are no right or wrong answers—this exercise is designed to increase awareness and help you identify areas for improvement.

- Do I know how much money comes into my household each month?
- Do I know where my money goes each month?
- Do I have an emergency fund with at least three to six months of living expenses?
- Am I carrying credit card debt from month to month?
- Am I saving consistently for retirement?
- Do I have adequate life, disability, and health insurance coverage?
- Do I have an up-to-date will, power of attorney, and beneficiary designations?
- Am I making financial decisions based on my goals or my emotions?
- Could I handle a $1,000 unexpected expense without borrowing money?
- If I continue on my current financial path, will I be where I want to be in five years?

Your Score

8–10 Yes Answers: Congratulations! You have built a strong financial foundation. Continue refining your plan and monitoring your progress.

5–7 Yes Answers: You're making progress, but there are opportunities to strengthen your financial position and increase your confidence.

0–4 Yes Answers: Don't be discouraged. Every financial journey starts with awareness. Focus on improving one area at a time and celebrate each step forward.

Chapter 3

The Math is Not Mathing

You know when you put on your best outfit, nice shoes, got the bag, and you wear your favorite perfume? You know how your joy seems to fill the space around you? That sweet aroma gets you compliments, and people can tell how you feel. It's okay. We all have our thing. But when you feel good about yourself, you make better decisions concerning yourself. Did you know that?

James Brown said: "I look good, I feel good, I smell good..." There is something about having a clean house, smelling clean air, and being in a clean environment that helps us to think and feel our best. Would you agree? I know once you have gotten those kitchen counters cleaned, you spot the mail. That stack of envelopes is such an eyesore, even if there are two or three pieces lying around. I believe we all love clean countertops.

So, what is a quick fix to get everything you don't want on your counter off? Place it into the junk drawer to deal with later. Some of us have a junk bowl which you toss items into also. Now, let's talk about your junk drawer. You know the drawer you have, like I do, in your kitchen where you toss anything random that you know you will need someday, just not sure for when, inside of.

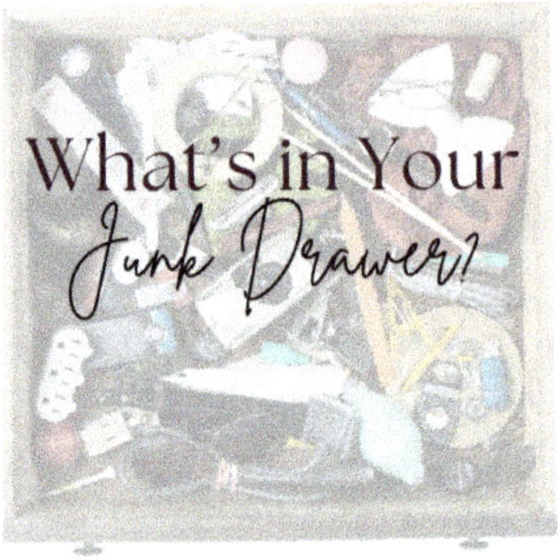

This drawer can hold mail, screws and bolts, and condiment packages. It is not uncommon for this drawer to hold important information you will need, like important documents, birth certificates, or other bills you don't want to lose. This drawer may often be overlooked and usually it is because we don't feel like dealing with what is in the drawer.

As parents, spouses, employees, business owners, or etc., we have a lot of things to do daily. It can be overwhelming to think about your future when you are really concerned with the here and now. So instead of us thinking of things we feel are for somewhere out in the future or that deal with money–too often, we shove it into this drawer.

I want to show that although this may feel like an easy fix, out of sight, out of mind, it is not how you want to operate in your finances or your life.

There are conversations that you will need to have. I know you probably know people who can hold hard feelings against someone for years and even decades. If only they had been uncomfortable and faced a scary conversation one time, they could have had peace for the rest of their lives.

Finances are like that, too! If you avoid looking at your credit, it will not get better. If you limit your vision and dreams because of the current score, you are settling for a life less than you deserve. Will it take work to get through the drawer and put things where they belong, yes. However, when you go through this drawer, you will have a clear path of execution that will simplify other aspects of your life.

So, what's in the drawer? Bills. I am sure you have electric bills, insurance, medical, or "surprise bills" in there. Question: Do you have a plan for how you will pay these bills? Even if you have the money, it is still good to assess your charges. When you look at your bills, there are a few things you should look for.

Bill Review:

- Check the dates. Sometimes, there are print errors with dates addresses, and there could be a mixup for the bill you are receiving.
- Check the usage. Is the usage normal? Are you consuming more services than other similar accounts? Can you reduce usage to

save money?
- Are you taking advantage of auto-pay bonuses? And paying your bill on time. Sometimes, improving your credit score can improve rates and options.

I would say here that you should improve your credit score. Bills that utilize your credit score, like car notes, houses, etc, can be adjusted or refinanced when you improve your scores to save money.

You want to analyze the items in your drawer and ask key questions for deciphering where things go and if you honestly need it. Some things in the junk drawer you don't need. You might have very old bills tucked in there. Bills that are paid. Has the drawer also become your filing system? It is good to keep documents for some time, especially for the IRS and other companies, but designate a place for that. You want to organize important documents and put them in a safe place.

What about how this drawer holds your spending receipts? I know most of us use our cards. How are spending cards impacting your spending? If you go to Forbes, Bankrate, Nerdwallet, or any other financial magazine and newspaper, you will find that we spend more when using credit cards versus cash. It is reported we spend 12-18% more when charging on credit cards than if we were paying with cash.

Is that percentage true for you? If you set out

envelopes with the exact cash for your budget, can you be disciplined not to spend a penny over? Literally, because you don't have it. Not everything in your bank account is available for spending. Sometimes, having those envelopes is the best way to control your spending if you need a nudge.

For some of us, this tip has helped us save, but this helpful tip does not prevent you from breaking the rules and taking out a card to charge what you saved. The next step I want you to do is go through your receipts. If you are not printing or keeping your receipts, I want you to save your receipts for everything you buy throughout the week.

What you will find might scare you. You don't realize spending $20 on food to eat a meal one time in the day is costing you $600 a month. Is it worth it? Do you have an income to maintain this kind of eating habit? Would you spend the $600 like this if you had the cash in an envelope, or would you cut back naturally because the amount seems like a lot?

Maybe it is not food, maybe it is coffee, clothes, alcohol, lottery, etc.. You get the point. When we purchase certain items that are privileged as if they are mandatory, we will try and justify this spending. We will say, I need coffee to get my day going. That may be true, have you considered buying a bag of your favorite coffee blend and making it at home? If you took your coffee budget, could you afford a nice machine, the coffee, and the ingredients you need to make a great cup of coffee?

The Math that is not Mathing

Most people spend $3 to $5 for a cup of coffee. If you multiply that budget over 30 days, it would quickly jump to $90 -$150. Could you buy a top brand, other ingredients, and a machine with that budget? Consider adding that price up for 3 months, that is $450! With that budget, could you now buy a nice coffee pot, cup, coffee, and ingredients? A scarier question: how much do you spend a year on coffee with these numbers? A whopping $1,800. What could you do with some discipline and designated time to make your coffee at home instead of buying it every day.

What money is leaving your pockets quickly because you haven't taken inventory of your spending? I know this is a sensitive topic, but we are going to jump a little deeper into your spending. There are two more areas we must look at that can creep up on us. Groceries. I know we all need food to eat breakfast, lunch, and dinner. But how many of us buy ready-made items?

I am not arguing about nutrition right now; however, it is very important. But when you have a mindset that cooking and eating should be done quickly, you may be tempted to rush through the process. In the grocery stores, they play music that keeps you calm and puts you in a comfortable state of being. In this state, you shop each aisle one by one. When you move slowly through the aisles, it is documented you spend more.

Why is that we spend more? Are we shopping with our eyes? Are we undisciplined to buy what we need from the list? How can you better your shopping experience and increase your discipline? You have to go through the receipts and see what you are spending on and then consider the math for the year. As you start looking at your receipts more and more, you will begin to see the pattern presented in your drawer.

When I first started my journey, and looking at my account from when I was 18 to now, I have become more conscious of my spending. As I started doing this work, like many of my clients, they see the value in days. It's amazing how our eyes open when we are hip to problems with a solution to solve it. This process can be applied to all areas in your life.

Just like you have a junk drawer to hold financial matters and items you don't want to deal with, your life might bear the same truth. I can say, "If I am the same 19-year-old at 48 with my approach to my finances, I should be concerned because there wasn't any growth." But how can I be certain I am different at 48 than when I was 19, unless I assess what is in my life drawer?

This junk drawer shows your perspective and what you value. If you check your receipts right now, do you value or see your true self? It is easy to say anything, but your actions must line up. Do you eat healthy to prove you love your body? Do you get rest at night? Do you take an hour out for yourself daily or once a day–even a half day a week to do something you enjoy?

Being a mom, wife, sister, aunt, employee, and employer, we can collect other people's receipts in our lives, can't we? People will give you their bills and try to make them yours. They will share their problems and make their lack of discipline your responsibility and your emergency too. But do you have boundaries? Can you say "no" and mean it? Is there power in your "no?" Who are you in your personal perspective?

Download the article "Hello Me: Finding Yourself" with the QR or visit the website.

Access Free Resources
Scan or Visit
latoyamaddox.com

I can tell you I am an empowered and confident woman, a feminist in that I have compassion and an outlook to help encourage women. I want you to understand that we have to protect ourselves and our identity from being trampled on. If you don't know what you want to accomplish, lack clear goals/dreams/plans, you will go with everyone else's ideas over your own. You will let others throw their junk in your drawer.

When you open that junk drawer, have you ever said, "I don't know how this got in here? Who did this?" I will admit to you, I have said that many times. When our lives are unorganized we cannot see when someone is dumping their junk on us. In my youth, there was a time when I was losing sight of my goals and losing money because I was allowing other people's needs and concerns to become mine. We can have a heart to give, but don't be compelled to give what you don't have.

If you need to spend time with yourself, stop giving that time to someone else. You are valuable and you do matter. Your dreams matter along with your saving goals and everything else. Not everyone intends on dumping on us, but many are guilty of it. Our children, spouse, parents, or anything and everyone else can be guilty of dumping on you. Set aside what you are budgeting to give, but don't give away what you need for yourself financially or otherwise.

It is tempting to say, "I got to make sure x, y, z is done. I don't have time this week or right now."

But putting off the necessary organization of this drawer can mean it gets so full it will not open. Sometimes, we get so busy doing stuff for others that we have no time for anything else. But don't allow your lifestyle to cancel out your priorities. What makes you happy? Don't get so busy making everyone else happy that you forget about yourself in the process. Or you don't know what you like anymore. You can lose sight of yourself very easily. Before you know it, you have cast yourself as an extra in your own movie.

But you must reel it in. Before you became a wife, you were first single. Before you were a mother, you were a young woman ready to take on the world. So take the time to get to know and love yourself. You are more than your responsibilities. Get back in touch with what gets you excited. If you have lost yourself, too much is in your drawer, now is the time to clean out the junk. Look at what is there and decide what must go to the shredder. Commit to making some life changes.

My favorite quote by Audre Lorde: "If I didn't define myself for myself, I would be crunched into other people's fantasies for me and eaten alive."
– Audre Lorde

Find yourself to design yourself. If you don't have a plan, someone else has one for you. If you don't plan for your well-being and your financial security, other companies and people have something in store for you. I want to help you more with an invaluable resource, this is a free resource entitled "Identifying and Eliminating Your Poor Financial Habits." If you are struggling with your finances or want to do more for yourself, I want you to get this resource and complete the activity.

Access Free Resources
Scan or Visit
latoyamaddox.com

Chapter 4

Comprehensive Plan

If you are out with your husband, sitting in the car, hanging out with friends, or your co-workers this situation is bound to come up. You know the big debate that happens when it is time to go and do something. Most people are polite enough to ask the group or the other person a solid question, "What would you like to eat?"

Growing up I didn't like the question because I wasn't too sure. For those of us where coming up with an answer is a challenge, is it because we honestly don't know? Are we tired of eating the same foods? Do we tend to go with what we know so we say, "Whatever you want is cool." Or do we really not have an answer and don't think twice about it.

Like so, in groups, when that same question is asked, there is usually one person who has something to say–at times a lot to say. That person who knows what they have been craving all day will speak, the one who is used to being the boss will voice their thoughts, and the one that is selfish. They don't all speak at once and not everyone in the group falls into one of these categories; but often the one that speaks first gets their choice. Unless, the second or third voice is more persuasive.

Either way, everyone in the group ends up going along with one of the vocal voices. If you never speak up for what you want, how will people ever get a chance to follow your vision? How will they know your plans, if you never share them? The worst, how can you direct your life if you allow everyone around you to speak for you.

Honestly, no person that loves you wants to make all the decisions and have you be the "yes man" or "yes woman." They value you and likewise your opinion and ideas. So if you never speak, what is the world missing? How much resentment are you building toward people because you refuse to speak up and they do? Not everyone is an attention hound, but if people around them don't engage in conversation and making decisions, these types of people will take the lead.

I want to encourage you to speak your mind even if it is not what everyone agrees to do. We need to normalize speaking when we have ideas and not overthinking. Too often, we don't speak because we are concerned or thinking what someone else thinks or would they like it. I know something I did in my first marriage that I regretted, I stopped talking.

I stopped saying how I felt and what I needed. It doesn't take a rocket scientist to predict the outcome–that created a wedge in the relationship.

In your life, how are you placing wedges in your relationships? How are you distancing relationships that should be comforting you and loving you back? There is a correlation between relationship satisfaction and financial security. What about your finances? How you value your relationships will cause you to grow or shrink. Meaning, you will either elevate your finances or deflate them with your habits and lifestyle.

If you are making poor habits in one area, it will leak over into other facets of your life. If you don't speak about where you want to eat, something yes that is simple. What confidence do you have to speak up about interests you love, if you may face rejection or people's opinions? It is a real fear many of us have, fearing the outcome and opinions of others.

The one thing I've noticed as I have gotten older and wiser in business is older people tend to speak their minds more. This applies in personal and business settings. As we get older, we get to a point where we don't care how others feel about everything we choose to do. There is a switch that clicks that says, "You know what, I am going to do this, and everyone will have to accept it."

Sometimes it is who we choose to marry, when we start our business, what we invest in, or how we raise our children, and other life decisions. You should hear sound wisdom, of course, but is it wise to allow fear and everyone else's opinions to scare you into doing nothing? Not moving forward with your dreams, plans, desires, or goals?

No, you don't owe anyone anything if you are choosing to improve your life. However, you do owe yourself truth. You must be to your own self truthful. When you can have confidence and boldness in how you feel about your ideas, you can encourage yourself when others don't agree or see your vision. The truth, not everyone will see it no matter what you do. Sometimes you have to step out and be the example that others see win for them to believe.

Stay encouraged if you are the first to make moves on your dreams and goals. Start speaking up about the life you want, start thinking the experiences you want to have! Sometimes we don't have an answer because we don't think about things we should. Don't avoid the hard questions because of the fear of failure or displeasing others. Another truth you will find as you live, you will displease or challenge someone at some point. Do it any way. Better yet: Do it scared!

I want to tell you not to retreat. For some, as you build your voice, it decreases their power and influence over you. Sometimes this influence is healthy, but too often it is manipulation and someone benefiting from your silence. Healthy relationships, will celebrate your growth not shun you for making progress in self-discovery.

I want to remind you to have a little or a lot more grace. Some of us have so much pressure to win, that we feel we cannot make a mistake. We are so busy we can't think about stuff that isn't primary to living life. If it is not bills, work, business, making money, spending money wisely, we can go blank. We may be guilty of abandoning the people around us because we are unavailable.

It is a hard reality to realize even though you are around people, you are not actively participating. When you are like this, although people love you, it can make you feel if you were not there would anyone notice? Give yourself grace. Those that love you, they will notice your presence and appreciate your input.

Another relatable example to show if you need to work on your voice and confidence is how you participate in groups. If you tend to be silent during group think sessions, you shouldn't. You could have the missing piece to solve the puzzle. No one will know if you don't vocalize your ideas. Don't assume that everyone at the table will fight your battles, either. Some battles are yours to fight, and to win in your finances and get serious about your dreams, is your battle.

A worthy battle you will have to fight is the urgency to want to be blameless if something goes wrong. Some people don't speak because if it doesn't work, or someone who spoke is wrong, they will get the backlash. Have you noticed how in a classroom setting when most of the class is uncertain of the answer, everyone is quiet? No one wants to talk and speak the wrong answer, because they know the class might laugh.

Are you afraid of people laughing at your plans, thoughts or ideas? Not speaking can be linked to not wanting to be the reason you fail. Have you noticed the people who don't like ordering their food? They will ask, "What's good here?" Not because they are curious, but they want to blame the waitress if the food is nasty, and say, "You told me this was good. It is not, I want something else."

Have you felt taken by someone selling you soup, as we say? We can go into arrangements thinking one thing and end with another. This can shape our thought patterns and make it difficult for us to see other ideas. It can make us afraid to invest because making money is often attached to making decisions that can go very well or terribly.

Don't fear being judged by others for your choices. Not a person alive has lived without scrutiny, even the Messiah had to deal with people and their thoughts concerning Him. Be open to accept the decisions you make that are good, but also the ones that cause you to learn. Most people don't mind receiving credit for the wins in their lives, but the born leaders must also become accountable to accept and learn quickly from their losses. If you choose to be silent so you can have someone else to blame when your choices fail, you could also release your chance to have the victory.

Fail fast and then pivot. You can always turn a challenge into a victory in your life. If you see a problem in your finances it is a chance for you to think differently. Don't avoid making decisions but learn to adapt. I cannot stress enough the importance of self-confidence when changing your financial projection.

I have to tell you that it wasn't until I took a step back and looked at what I wanted and saw where I could improve that I accomplished my goals. Yes, I made choices many didn't make at ages in my life, and those decisions lead to great outcomes. In my case, I made a choice to pick my high school and not let a system, or administrator belittle my wishes. I learned the power of my voice young, but you too can learn the power of "no."

Sometimes the answer is not cute and easy to deliver, I had to go against my mother and other adults who were professionals sent to help me make better decisions. They failed me as it pertained to helping me get what I wanted out of life. Some people in your life meant to help you, might be holding you in limbo because of their fears. When my divorce happened, there was nothing to figure out, because I knew why and when it ended. Sticking around was only delaying the inevitable. A change was necessary.

Ripping off the band-aid is at times a necessary part of life. Making hard decisions gets easier when you have a taste of your power, and are in control of your confidence. When something doesn't work, consider what boundaries you need to establish. The resentment I had in my first marriage was because I felt it was one-sided. The truth, it was. I could have spoken up much sooner, but I didn't. Not digging deeper into it because that's the past and as I said, there was nothing to figure out.

Don't waste too much time thinking on things that could have been, focus on where you are and what you want today and also for the future. As you do that, making the necessary changes becomes a lot easier. See, if you need more money to save and have the retirement you need, be prepared to make a life choice like going back to college if that is necessary. Others may have to start a business and do the necessary prep work for that to be successful at the foundation to permit the best growth in the future. Both of these choices are a choice to invest in you!

How can you develop a mindset to stay in school when everything is coming at you? Marriage doesn't take a break, children, life, or your job. Learning how to establish healthy boundaries and to speak up is critical.

If you need a Comprehensive Plan I can help. We all need to be prepared for our financial future so life events are not so difficult. The more you know, the more prepared you can be for life events. It will rain on the just and the unjust, so you better have an umbrella!

Access Free Resources
Scan or Visit
latoyamaddox.com

Moving towards your goals is a process. Remember, Rome wasn't built in a day. The road to financial independence is a process. No one got the retirement they wanted by putting money away one time. Most people have a consistent schedule and way of thinking that builds wealth over time. So, have some grace. If you feel you are starting late, after a divorce, or things are irreversible, take note. You can change your finances no matter how much money you have today and what you do for a living.

To make the greatest impact, you may have to dig deeper, find your voice, and dare to dream. Dreaming is something we do as children, but when we become adults, life seems to snuff that out doesn't it? Children have the freedom to think big picture, unrealistically, and out of the box. They are not restricted and have the gift or abundant thinking.

When I say to give yourself grace, I mean for you to give yourself what you give to others. If people ask, "What do you want?" Allow yourself to speak up like you do for others. When others tell you I cannot do this or that for you, don't get mad, think that's a healthy boundary to be able to say "no." Your perspective is everything. Like how children can dream and see things a different way, try to apply that to your circumstances. Life is long and it can be short.

Some people fear going to school or starting a business because of the "long time" it will take to get a degree or achieve success. I want to ask you, or those who think like this, where will you be in 5 or 10 years if you don't go back to school? Can you imagine most of these people will be working and doing the same thing 5 and 10 years from now, getting the same results. Albert Einstein said it best "Insanity is doing the same thing and expecting a different result."

Your life will not change if you don't change your mind to change your finances. Do you know you cannot save your way out of poverty? If you think stacking a few bucks away into a savings account monthly will save you, I am sad to tell you it will be appreciated but super slow. Life moves faster than saving accounts grow. There are instruments you can use to help make more money off your money. Understanding the beauty of compounding interest, is non-negotiable. Financial literacy is a must. Learning how money works will give you the confidence needed to grow, build, and protect your wealth.

I am frequently asked, "How can I stabilize my life when one thing after another keeps happening?" My answer, "Life will never be put on hold. But we can position ourselves to overcome most of our challenges when we make better choices. In the beginning it is a learning curve, but give yourself grace Riding a bicycle takes you falling off and getting back on before you get it. Same thing with investing and developing a workable comprehensive plan."

Yes, reaching your financial goals is difficult if your foundation is weak. But most people's problem with making, having, and keeping money is not that they don't work hard enough. It is not that they don't have good intentions, or even that they don't want it bad enough. It is their ability to change their money mindset. It is the commitment you need to financial education, maintaining basic financial principals, and or going that extra mile, even while the rest is happening that helps to make financial stable people.

Anyone that has accomplished a solid financial foundation in finances, they will all tell you they had to sacrifice and put in work and effort. Money didn't rain from the sky, it was built, and cultivated. No one is given donations to people because you have a desire for financial freedom. We have to dig deep and some of us, deeper than others, to achieve this goal of financial success. I have to tell you it may feel unfair, it may bring some resentment to see what you have to do because your parents didn't have a comprehensive plan.

How do you respond when you feel slighted about your condition? Do you think, work and pray your way out of it? Prayer without works is dead. So if you want to change your life, you are going to have to do more than speak it for it to manifest. You need to get mentally tough and work smart! Long hours, multiple jobs, and having no sleep is not always the way to change your life. It may just lead to burn out. Education is the ticket to understanding how to work smarter and hire the right team of professionals to fill in the knowledge gaps to help you that knows more than you.

You are not a fool to pay money to learn something you don't know. It is foolish to keep investing in something you don't understand or know because you can't quantify the value or determine how much you save or have lost. To rehire a new contractor at full price because the cheaper company made mistakes, costs you more in the long run. If you get what you pay for, it might be best to pay for what you want.

As a small business owner, you have to know how to take inventory of your products and look over your accounts. Many people rob companies blind because they are not looking at the numbers. Unfortunately, many stores close because of theft every year. Fraud is also ramped in our personal lives, so make it a habit to take time and look over your investments.

But don't stop there, look at what else is being stolen out of your life? Are you losing your time in a dead-end job, relationship, or functions that eat your time and keep you distracted from accomplishing your goals? You have to wake up from your slumber and constant rhythm of life to recognize

Life Wheel Exercise

Financial success means different things to different people. Before creating goals for your money, it's important to understand where you are in the areas of life that matter most.

Rate your level of satisfaction in each area below on a scale of 1 to 10, with 1 being "Needs Significant Improvement" and 10 being "Thriving."

Life Area - Score (1-10)	
Financial Health	____
Physical Health	____
Mental & Emotional Well-Being	____
Family Relationships	____
Friendships & Social Life	____
Career or Business	____
Personal Growth & Learning	____
Spiritual Life	____
Fun & Recreation	____
Community & Giving Back	____

Reflection Questions

1. Which area received your highest score?
2. Which area received your lowest score?
3. Are there any areas where your financial decisions are helping you thrive?
4. Are there any areas where your financial decisions may be holding you back?
5. If you could improve just one area over the next 12 months, which would have the greatest positive impact on your overall quality of life?

Your Next Step

Choose one area that needs attention and write down one action you can take this week to move it forward. Remember, meaningful change rarely comes from dramatic transformations. It comes from small, consistent actions repeated over time.

My experience as a financial planner has taught me that money is rarely the real goal. The goal is the life that money helps you create. When your financial plan supports your values, relationships, health, and purpose, you're not just building wealth—you're building a life worth living.

the things that are keeping you from achieving personal and financial success.

Up next, we are going to talk about how you can position your life to improve from wherever you are. Improvement just like success is relevant. If you are not in the same place in a year as where you are today, that is good. Celebrate your large and small victories. They all help you along your journey to have grace, and keep moving forward at any pace.

Chapter 5

A Glimpse of What I Learned

How many of us learned the hard way that when you finish high school life isn't set on cruise control to take care of you? I was ambitious, I had goals for my life, but I wasn't educated on what I needed to do to provide for myself. I knew I needed to earn an income to provide, but I was unaware of how money worked exactly.

What about you? How much did you know about financial literacy when you exited high school? Did you have a game plan on how to take care of yourself? Were you also forced to enter adulthood and choose between working to afford a place to live and food to eat or attending college?

I didn't start with a solid foundation. My grandmother was in insurance and she was well off considering all things for black families during this time. My mother wanted good things for me, but she was not certain of how I would obtain them. She believed in great things but didn't have the road map on how to get there.

That was the first thing I wanted to do for the clients I served. I wanted to build a road map that will help educate them on financial literacy, and show them what their futures could look like. My mom did have something right, after I finished high school, me and my boyfriend moved into our first apartment together. We lived together and things seemed to be going well. But we just could not gain any momentum financially.

After some deep reflection, we discovered something was missing from the picture. Our vision was not coming to life because we were focusing on the present. The first step I had to do, that I encourage you to do also, is to take inventory of your skillset. When experience is not on your side, you need to leverage your talents to achieve your goals.

I needed a higher paying job if I wanted to be able to take care of myself. I grew up in Chicago like many of my friends and family. I had the same culture in my community about money, but my grandmother always wanted more. In that sense I took after her because when she told me she was headed to Georgia for better opportunities I was on board with going with her.

My grandmother was helpful in helping me get a job at a well-known insurance company, Travelers. The ladies who I worked with were all older than me and I loved being under their mentoring. They not only trained me for the job I had as a self report works compensation audit processor, but also taught me work ethic and valuable corporate lessons. I was being molded to follow in my grandmother's footsteps and moving to Georgia. Travelers had a Georgia location and I applied for a transfer that I was sure to get.

Have you ever had a plan that seemed to fall through the cracks? I went to the interview knowing I knew the material so I was confident I would get a promotion in transferring and landing this job. The glitch, I had to take a typing test to type 50 wpm and I failed. Because I didn't pass that test, I couldn't get the job. Actually, they didn't even interview me. I never made it past the keyboard room. I remember leaving the Travelers office and telling the woman who let me out that not to worry because I had another job interview lined up.

Motto: Always have a plan B. Of course, I didn't fly all the way from Chicago to Atlanta for one job interview. My grandmother had a done business with a local insurance agency, Phoenix Associates. She let them know I was coming down and they offered to interview me during my time in Atlanta.

I interviewed with Phoenix Associates and was offered a job the same day. I was 19 years old. Landing the job this offered me an opportunity to start a new career, I learned to type, and started making good money. I could afford to be single, happy, and life was good again. This was a major success for me. I thought I had "made it" until my new co-worker (turned bestfriend) Neidra hit me with a gut punch of reality.

I remember going with the flow of my day and Neidra and I went on break. Neidra was smoking a cigarette. In 1997 she was in her 40s and she said, "So what are you going to do?" I looked at her a bit puzzled, "I am working. Got a job, an apartment, I am straight."

She flicked ashes from her cigarette and said, "Everyone I know that is about something has a degree. Where is yours? You are doing good today, but what about in the future?" She was right. I was making good money so I forgot about college and getting my degree. I took the ACT in school and did well, but I felt my current streak of luck with success meant maybe I didn't need to make it a priority.

I am glad I took her advice. I not only went to college, but I came up with a plan to make college work with my current job. I worked full time during the day and went to school full time at night. I needed to continue to support myself financially so this was the only way for me to accomplish my goal. I first enrolled into a community college in Kennesaw while I worked at Phoenix Associates for the first year. Then I transfers to Georgia State University for the remaining 3 years to finish. Prelaw with African American Studies was my intended major and minor, but I didn't see how it directly connected to what I was doing.

Have you ever done something because it seemed safe even though it was not you? I respect law and love what people can accomplish in the field, but my passion was not in law. I love working with people in the African American community, helping to balance scales and bring representation to industries we are not heavily present in. I still get to impact my community and culture by doing something I love. I thought to become more resourceful with connecting my interest. So, after I earned my 4 year degree, I had 6 years of experience in insurance. I was ready to elevate in my career.

Around 2002, I researched in the Career Almanacs of what will be a top job for the future, I saw that a financial advisor came up frequently. Certified Financial Planner was the top designation to have in the field at that time. Next, I looked at what it took and what kind of experience I must have to enter this field. I already worked in life and health insurance, but our firm did not offer financial planning. I quickly got excited and then inspired to suggest offering this bridge to connect our clients to more services and boost insurance sales.

I had a meeting with my boss (Robert Marcus) and got more than I planned for. He was not only impressed with my idea, he told me he would cover the costs of my education. I obtained the Certified Financial Planner designation in 2005. This gave me the idea to start my own company. Sometimes we can dream, then we learn to dream bigger! I was not only going to finish a degree that was relevant to my here and now, I also had the opportunity to launch my own business! The angels were singing in my ears "Haaaa."

I was happy to turn this corner and life seemed again to be going better than well. I started my company Infinity Financial. In 2005 my business started offering financial planning, taxes, and investment management, and I continued to do life and health insurance through Phoenix Associates.

Life wasn't just about business and my education, I also was in a romantic relationship. I got married and had my first child in 2011. The marriage was strained for numerous reasons, so ultimately, it did not work out 7 years later. I became a single mom operating my own business. I became my own ideal client which is how I work so well in this client demographic.

Starting a business is not just about what you want to do for people, but how you have compassion and work to find solutions for the people you want to serve. Most of my clients are women who are going through divorce, the death of a spouse, single parents, or women in transition. My heart is to treat these women how I wanted to be treated when I was in their shoes. I believe in what I do and I want to improve the lives of all of my clients who trust me to serve them

I had a pie in the sky point-of-view, but that didn't mean I did not face challenges in this industry. Most people buy from people who look like them. My ideal client, although they shared the same situation, did not share the same ethnic background. Race played a role in the growth of my company because people are wired to buy from those who look like them.

Insurance for a long time was a white male dominated industry, I was neither white nor male. I had my work cut out for me to make it under these terms but I was up for the challenge. I refused to allow race to be a reason I was not able to achieve my goals. I wanted to refute any reason someone could have not to work with me, so I returned back to school for my Executive MBA. I was promoted to COO of Phoenix Associates and an equity partner.

My story is not everyone's story. I had a great company that saw my potential and wasn't afraid to invest in my growth and honored their commitment to grow with the company. My practice has grown over the years substantially and I do more investments, wills, trusts, and estate planning than insurance.

My life is proof that anyone who is willing to think outside of the box can take hold of their financial picture and work it to their good. No matter what it looks like right now, I can help you structure and transition your financial endeavors to grow with your future needs and demands. I mentioned earlier to look at your skill set. Most people coming to me feel they don't have enough money to financially plan for their future.

I ask every new client, can you afford not to do this? Where will you be in 3 months, 6 months, or a few years if this doesn't change? Lastly, can you do this yourself or do you want my knowledge and help?

I am a firm believer that what you need to transform your life you have. You are smart, you have goals, and the only question you have to answer is, "Are you willing to take action and implement the steps you need to get there?" You cannot remain comfortable and find your way to financial freedom. You cannot merely dream about starting your business, having financial freedom, or living the life you want without planning for it.

Your road to prosperity may include starting a company, acting on a business idea, repositioning assets, or some other endeavors. If you have a skill that is transferable you have unlimited income. Skills are marketable. You just have to build up your nerve and be willing to put yourself out there and promote yourself to tap into your full potential.

Flip the switch and accumulate the money you need. If you need to earn extra money to afford your life, look for someone or something to encourage you. My daughter lit that fire in me. Also,look for who or what is putting demands on your finances. For me, education was the key for me to earning more money and opening new opportunities. Don't be afraid to invest in yourself and potential.

Most families are two or three generations from poverty. Which means many of us were left to our own to figure out life and finances. You do not have to follow that same life pattern.

When I was younger, I didn't think twice about estate planning even though I worked in the industry. I was the client I was sent out to attract, educate, and help empower.

This industry is more than a job and career for me, it is my passion and mission personified to help impact the world. I am building a legacy that includes helping other women and families secure their futures. I am a small part of a big picture and

50/30/20 Rule

What I Learned from the 50/30/20 Rule

One of the first budgeting frameworks I encountered was the 50/30/20 rule. The concept is simple: allocate 50% of your income to needs, such as housing, utilities, insurance, and groceries; 30% to wants, such as dining out, entertainment, and travel; and 20% to savings, investing, and debt repayment.

To apply the rule, start by calculating your monthly take-home pay. Next, categorize your spending into needs, wants, and savings. Compare your current spending to the 50/30/20 targets and make adjustments where necessary. The goal isn't perfection—it's awareness and intentionality.
While I appreciated the simplicity of the framework, I quickly learned that personal finance is rarely one-size-fits-all. Some seasons of life may require more than 50% for necessities, while others may allow you to save far more than 20%.

What the rule taught me wasn't the exact percentages; it was the importance of giving every dollar a purpose. Whether your priority is paying off debt, building an emergency fund, saving for retirement, or investing for future goals, the real value comes from creating a spending plan that aligns with your life and your values.

Today, I view the 50/30/20 rule as a starting point rather than a destination. The best budget isn't the one that follows a formula perfectly—it's the one that helps you consistently make progress toward the life you want to build.

that brings me joy. I want you to find that for yourself in what you do. I want you to work for what you want but also invest smart so you have more as you age.

We all know government funded programs are likely going to be non-existent or require you to have zero assets to qualify for any benefits. If you want to have something to give to your children, you need to start planning now.

I my lifetime, I've meet people who have refused to transform their lives. Their street address hasn't changed and for many of them, neither has their financial picture. If you want more, you have to invest in yourself and in other people. For some people, a completely new environment may be necessary.

To get something you want, I want to be clear, you will have to leave your comfort zone. You will have to be committed to stop behaviors that prove to be a hindrance. I had to read books, attend college, and grow through experience for what I can help my clients leap frog to learn. I escaped the traps of my birth and explored the world. I wanted to bring the environments I was reading about in books into my life. Then, most importantly, I wanted to help others do the same.

Clients with something to protect: children, assets, money, savings, and securing their future contact me for help. When you think about transitioning from a job, are making decisions about your 401k, or other financially impactful decisions like marriage, buying a house or car, do you think of contacting your financial advisor? Would it surprise you if I told you that my clients call me whenever they are making big or financial impactful decisions? I don't tell my clients what to do, but I advise them on what to consider. Who do you call when you are making your decisions? Are they qualified to give you quality feedback, or merely an opinion that could lead you in the wrong direction?

What are some ways we solicit advice from people about critical decisions in our lives? It could be asking an unmarried person about marriage. Asking a person without a 401k about yours, or people who are just not where you are nor do they comprehend the question, to answer your money questions. A financial planner's job is to help you achieve your financial and life goals by walking with you through the tough questions to help you make informed decisions. We cannot be all heart and no brain. Striking a balance between the two is essential for life transformation.

You want to build a quality relationship with your financial planner because you need to talk to them about your life goals and mapping it out. I had to put everything I wanted on paper when I started my journey so I know how you feel and I can help.

A Bible verse I absolutely love, "Write the

vision and make it plan so that others can see it and do it." The map is not just for you, it is for everyone concerning you. You are making provisions for them and yourself when you write down the vision. If you own property and assets, or anything, don't be afraid of a conversation about how to safeguard what you-have.

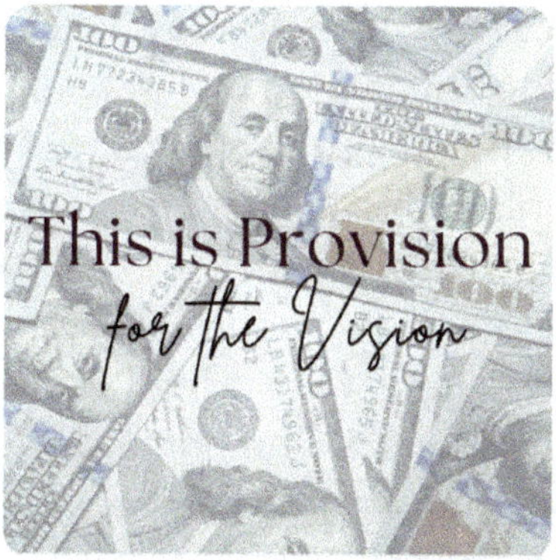

Before you marry, have a conversation to lay everything out to see what you both have together and respectfully, separately.

Don't have a junk drawer that you throw all of your cares of life into without organization. This method of arranging your life is not what anyone should advise you. Being able to fish out what you need when you need it, only to find it is incomplete, messed up from a ketchup package, is not the way to protect your family.

Try to get organized so it all makes sense before life happens. Saving bonds, checking accounts, savings accounts, 401k, IRAs, 529 plans, life insurance, etc all piled into a file. I create an Asset Map for all of my clients as an introductory first meeting–and believe it or not, we all have line items to include.

Yes there can be room for improvement and that is fine, but don't skip this step thinking there is nothing to your life. The asset map helps to show you all of your financial assets/documents on one page and how they work together. It can also encourage to create and have a game plan for finances.

As I grew in this field, I took a natural liking to career development coaching. One thing I loved about starting my own business, I eliminated the pressure of getting fired. I am not pressured to sell anything each month, so I can work in the best interest of my clients. I choose what I do and no one tells me what to do.

I have total freedom over my life and I love it. When working with my clients, I want them to be free to live and enjoy life on their terms. During our calls, I look for solutions and point out patterns and

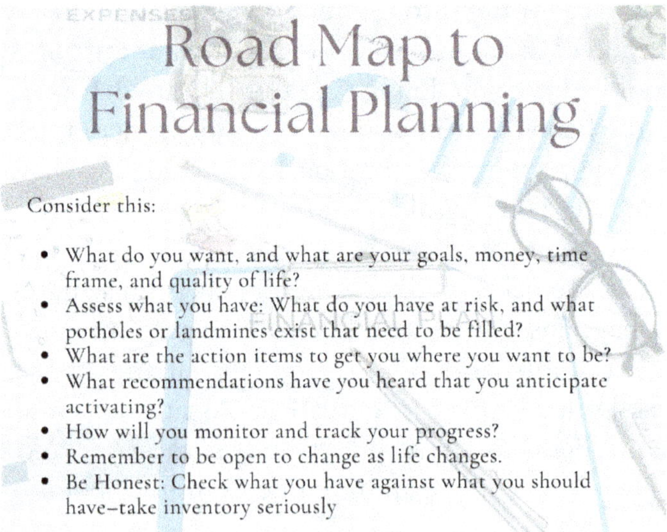

areas of concern with risk management focusing on: assets, retirement, health insurance, disability, and everyday checking and saving accounts.

People are creatures of habits, good or bad. We don't do things contrary to how we may sometimes respond "just because." We have a reason behind it all. The reason doesn't have to be complex, it can be as simple as that was how I was taught. This is all I know, or this is what I am comfortable doing. We can surely like things that are not good for us and give excuses for it before having a "Come to Jesus Moment," can't we?

I want to ease your fears or anxiety about financial planners. We are not here to make your life difficult but demonstrate how you can live now and enjoy your tomorrow. Financial planning isn't about sacrificing everything you enjoy today for a better tomorrow. It's about finding the balance between living well now and preparing wisely for the future.

Yes there are probably many things that ultimately need to be fixed but we don't expect you to throw it all at you in one meeting or in a month. It takes years to build rock solid habits so I ask that you be patient with yourself as you work to make changes.

I wrote a book called the "Smart Money Moves Playbook" that many of my clients order regardless of whether they work with me or not because they got to a point where they had to change their lives. They needed to understand their relationship with money and why they spend hey way they do. They needed to ultimately understand their relationship with money.

Understanding a key take-away from the book, you will see the patterns in how you spend money and make decisions concerning money. This rule of thumb will help you begin your journey and scale you up to where you want to be financially. If you know your money picture needs to change, you have to change your mind on how you see money. Changing your mind on money will change your life!

I know we think there are some difficult and hard facts we have to learn about life, but some of the most simple things have proven to be the most helpful over my years. You don't have to be the smartest in the room but know what you bring to the table. If your strong suit is not saving, you don't have to get married for that. You can have an advisor to help you on the way. Some of the reasons we get married are financial. But a husband might not be what you need but discipline.

I know that a book or changing your mindset about money is not the sexy answer we want, but if you want to change your life, you will make changes that are tangible and only you can do. You have to understand why you say "yes" or "no." Every day you are asked questions and have to say what you will buy, except, and how you will invest in your next decision. The answers you give are either opening or closing doors for you. So, be sure to open the right doors that lead to where you want to go.

Similarly to how there are love languages, there are also money spending languages. In my book, Financial Playbook, your money personality is defined depicting how and why we spend money. You can be a spend thrift, saver, money hoarder, and so forth. Determine your language and uncover how you can get unstuck from your financial challenges.

If you know you need someone to step you through the process, take the bootcamp. Next chapter we are going to talk about smart money moves that lead to your financial success.

What's Your Money Language

Circle the answer that best describes you.

1. You receive an unexpected $1,000 bonus. What is your first thought?
A. "I should save or invest this."
B. "I've earned a treat or experience."
C. "I can finally pay off some bills."
D. "How can I use this to make more money?"

2. When making a major purchase, you usually:
A. Research every detail before deciding.
B. Buy what feels right and fits your lifestyle.
C. Worry about whether you can afford it.
D. Think about its long-term value or return.

3. Which statement sounds most like you?
A. I feel secure when my savings are growing.
B. Money is meant to be enjoyed.
C. I often feel stressed about money.
D. I am always looking for opportunities to build wealth.

4. What is your biggest financial challenge?
A. Being too cautious.
B. Spending on things I enjoy.
C. Feeling overwhelmed by financial decisions.
D. Taking on too many financial projects at once.

5. Which financial goal excites you the most?
A. Building a strong emergency fund.
B. Traveling and creating memories.
C. Becoming debt-free.
D. Achieving financial independence.

What's Your Money Language

Your Results

Mostly A's – The Security Seeker
You value stability and peace of mind. Saving comes naturally, but be careful not to let fear keep you from enjoying your money and pursuing opportunities.

Mostly B's – The Experience Builder
You see money as a tool to enjoy life and create memories. Your strength is living in the present. Your challenge is balancing enjoyment with long-term planning.

Mostly C's – The Protector
You want financial security but may feel anxious or uncertain about money. Building knowledge, a spending plan, and small financial wins can help increase your confidence.

Mostly D's – The Wealth Builder
You are focused on growth, opportunity, and creating a lasting legacy. Your challenge is remembering that wealth is not just about accumulation—it's also about using money to support the life you want to live.

Chapter 6

Your Money Traps

So why do we leave traps? What would be the purpose of trying to lay a scheme, plan, or physical trap to catch someone or somebody? Often, traps are irresistible decisions that almost seems foolish not to make at the time.

There is a huge difference between opportunity and money traps. I want to transition the subject and focus more on your financial growth stories so I will introduce case studies I have worked on over the years to give you an idea of how financial management and services can benefit your life. I know we think we can make it and just budget our money to stay a float, but how many of you know that saving money in a bank is a trap?

Some of the lowest rates of interest are paid on regular savings accounts. Yes, saving is better than spending, but investing is better than saving. However, improper investing can leave you in worse financial shape. So how do you navigate around the money traps to keep you afloat when life throws a curve ball your way?

You have to get smart about your money. You have to be willing to learn what you do not know and not just hear it, but also follow it. Step outside your shell and open up to the leading of professionals who know a lot about money, spending, and how the financial system works against you. A good financial planner is going to adapt a plan to your situation and not just force you into a cookie cutter on how you can save money.

Yes, there are percentages and recommendations for how to allocate your money we can all learn from, but what if a major life event happens and you cannot follow the rule? What if you don't make enough to cover your expenses let alone having money in the budget to hire a professional for guidance. I want to encourage you that if you have a mindset or a will to solve your problems, they can be solved no matter what it looks like.

Take for example my Case Study 1.

Divorce Recovery and Financial Independence

When people transitioned in life either from being single to married, or married to divorce, it is a huge adjustment. It is even more stressful, painful, and emotional when you are in a divorce and also have to worry about income and assets being divided. Case Study 1, was a six-figure earning Marketing Executive working for a firm. She was happily married for several years to a man who also secured a high earning position, let's say in tech.

The two of them were building together and life happened. The home had a breakdown and the two of them became estranged and ultimately decided to part ways. During this process, a six-figure divorce ensued between the pair and money became the bigger issue than love. I know we have heard it said that money breaks up a lot of marriages. I want to introduce that money complicates a lot of divorces.

Before you even get a chance to argue about money, assets, and other benefits, you have to foot the bill for an attorney. When dealing with large sums of income it is extremely to your advantage to hire a paid lawyer. Lawyers do help win cases and if you think of representing yourself, no matter how well you speak and can prepare an argument, it can be hard to win everything you should have not knowing the system.

Similarly, after a large divorce or financial change you should call in a financial planner. When Case Study 1 came to me, she was emotionally broken, drained, and was not making the best decisions financially. She was trying to heal and she was buying anything that could distract her from what she was going through. Having discipline to know when to stop spending is a game we all play.

I remember when I purchased a purse for $400. You would have thought I whipped out my credit card to purchase the bag or cash. I did neither. I didn't pull out a card to buy to get points, I pulled out gift cards and got something I really liked. You see the point system on cards is meant to encourage you to spend. The credit card companies know the game of dangling something you want out there and giving you the means to buy it now and not plan for it. They hope you spend and buy up the world so you can be sand bagged with interest to pay it off, paying triple and quadruple scale to break even.

I had to look at Case Study 1 and assess what she needed in the moment and help her to get a plan to reel it all in. To be a good financial planner, it is not just about looking at a person's money, but looking at the person's needs. She needed a few things and had a few major problems. After our initial consultation, I wrote down a few bullets that would help us formulate a path forward to make smart money move decisions. Her case was like this:

Problems:

- Unfamiliarity with managing a seven-figure divorce settlement.
- No clear plan for retirement savings post-divorce.
- Emotional stress clouding financial decisions.

When you are unfamiliar with anything it will cost you something to get caught up to speed. You can pay a professional on the front, or you can pay the consequences of not paying someone on the backend. When we think we can get something for nothing we are not making smart money moves. We have to consider what we want to have and what is the best path forward to obtain it. She didn't know what she was doing and her plans forward were now blurry considering she didn't plan to be alone in planning for retirement. Her retirement had been divided or severed at the same time as her divorce was unfolding.

When life is happening fast, try not to make any long term decisions. Don't look to buy a car, house, or expensive gifts, but try with all your might to maintain or even pull back on spending. Prepare for what may come as much as you can and try not to worry. I knew we had to come up with a plan for her retirement savings post-divorce so that was the second thing we focused on. The third thing that had to be addressed was her emotional stress.

We had to deal with her emotional distress because that was causing her to make poor decisions. We could get going in the right direction, and one or a few purchases would derail it all. She needed a professional to deal with her emotions so I could focus on my job, managing her money and future financial picture. Managing money is a skill and it is a profession that professionals are trained to perform.

So, what was a snapshot of how I helped Case Study 1 through her divorce?

Solution:

- Created a detailed post-divorce financial roadmap.
- Consolidated her assets, opening a solo 401(k) and a taxable brokerage account.
- Collaborated with a therapist to help her detach emotionally from financial decisions.
- Implemented a sustainable budget and a plan to invest her settlement with an asset allocation strategy for growth and security.

Problems can be simplified when we are able to step back from them and have the guidance of a professional to help direct our path.

But what about scenarios that feature money

traps? Transitions are inevitable and we don't control when a relationship will end to a certain degree. Life happens to us all, does it not? But what about money traps we walk into that causes our financial picture to derail? Let's continue this journey and find a solution to help you avoid your money traps.

There are habits you have, that I once had, that entrap you in the snares of financial ruin. Good news, I am going to give you a few pointers on how I got a few clients out of money traps and if you need help, how I can help you too with Smart Money Moves!

Breaking the Debt Cycle for a Single Mom

Case Study 2 came into my office because she was tired of the life she had to live. She was a single mom very much in a position of robbing Peter to pay Paul. She relied on credit cards as her emergency fund and it would appear she didn't have a strong budget or strategy for how to make her money work for her. Life happened and she was responding to

life's demands but she was not growing or accomplishing her goals in most areas of her life.

She wanted to spend more time with her children, buy a house, invest, and save more money all of which wasn't happening. In our initial conversation, she had to be honest with me so I could find a way forward that would work for her current financial picture. So what were the money traps and solutions I ascertained from our first meeting?

Problems:

- Reliance on credit cards for emergencies.
- Lack of a clear savings strategy.

Solution:

- Debt Management: Created a debt snowball plan, starting with her smallest credit card balances to build momentum.
- Emergency Fund: Set up a high-yield savings account and automated small monthly contributions.
- Budget Restructure: Shifted spending by identifying non-essential expenses (e.g., streaming subscriptions, dining out) and redirecting funds toward her financial goals.

Empowerment: Partnered with her to develop a side hustle offering tutoring services, providing additional income for her savings and debt repayment.

Yes, to get out from underneath debt you will have to work! She picked up a side hustle which was part of her desire to have her own business and made it work for her needs. A side hustle shouldn't just be a money pit, it has to also perform. We had to consolidate her debt and help her to manage debt better. We started with the smallest debt and paid it off in full–and we didn't fill up the creditline when it was cleared.

Clearing debt is not removing debt then replacing it with new debt. She needed a better budget to ensure she didn't do that. It required her to pull back from non-essential spending and focus on her goal of being debt free. I know cutting out subscriptions, eating out, and buying things you like can be tough in the beginning, but it will eliminate stress in the long run.

So what were the results of our actions for Case Study 2?

Result:
Case Study 2 eliminated her credit card debt in 18 months, established a $5,000 emergency fund, and started contributing to her 403(b) plan.

She got out of her money pit and was able

to stabilize her life for the first time. Some of us didn't come from a balanced home with direction on estate planning and budgeting. We didn't have the luxury of ever feeling secure but we lived in a constant state of reacting to problems and bills. Establishing a financial plan brings a new way of living to the forefront if you are willing to endure the changes in the beginning. My Case Study's life is happier, her children spend more time with her, she has accomplished many of her goals, and now she knows she has a plan to retire not only debt free but can live off her investments!

Wouldn't that be nice to not have to work every day of your youthful life? Lifestyle is one of the biggest money traps you can step into. When we believe we are entitled to something and spend our money to have it, we can find ourselves digging the hole deeper into financial debt. I've worked with many clients who earned good incomes but found themselves struggling financially because their lifestyles had expanded beyond their means. Travel, vacations, shopping, and entertainment can provide temporary happiness and distraction from life's challenges. But when spending becomes the solution to every problem, it often creates bigger problems down the road. Lasting financial security comes from finding a balance between enjoying life today and preparing for tomorrow.

Eliminating Financial Stress for a Dual-Income Couple

Let's look at Case Study 3, a married couple with two teen boys. With children we know the bills will funnel in for some of everything but school, sports, utilities, food, clothing, shoes, and then the fun stuff like vacations and spending time together can trickle the bill up a lot more. This couple were working professionals so they made great money but they lived a lifestyle that left them financially poor. With the strain of finances the couple was under a lot of stress and worried constantly on paying for their boys schooling.

So let's take a quick glance at the issue for this family.

Money Traps:

- Living paycheck to paycheck despite a six-figure combined income.
- Overextended on luxury car leases and frequent vacations.

Solution:

- Lifestyle Audit: Conducted a cash flow analysis to identify "invisible leaks" in their budget.
- Expense Prioritization: Helped them trade their leased vehicles for pre-owned cars, cutting monthly expenses by $800.
- Savings Strategy: Automated contributions

to a Roth IRA and a 529 college savings plan.
- Communication: Facilitated a budgeting workshop for the couple to align their financial goals and priorities.

Living paycheck to paycheck can happen at any income level. Spending beyond a budgeted amount on lifestyle can leave anyone broke no matter how much you make. A debt mindset can be in any income level, so having more doesn't always point to making more, if you will only spend it. I had to reel this in and quickly.

Having nice things and living luxurious is nice, but it comes at a price. You have to do a lifestyle audit and identify if there are any invisible leaks in your budget. Are you overleveraged with the purchase of a particular car, house, vacation, etc. You want to prioritize your expenses also. Everything is not a priority. By becoming more practical with their car leases, I was able to save them $800 monthly. That is almost $10,000 a yr $9600 to be exact!

Of course, saving is part of the plan and putting away money for college funds. With two teen boys, they were going toward a double whammy of college expenses and now was the time to prepare for the financial turbulence up ahead. We cannot prepare to make our children happy only for the here and now, we have to also consider the future and balance that too.

The result of my changes were instantly seen and greatly impacted their life.

Result:

Michael and Andrea reduced their monthly expenses by $1,500, built a six-month emergency fund within a year, and felt less stressed about funding their children's college education.

Common Money Mistakes

Most money mistakes aren't caused by a lack of intelligence. They're often driven by emotions, habits, and beliefs we may not even realize are influencing our decisions. Understanding these common pitfalls can help you avoid them and make more intentional financial choices.

Lifestyle Creep

One of the most common financial traps is lifestyle creep. As your income increases, your spending rises right along with it. A bigger paycheck turns into a bigger house, a nicer car, more subscriptions, and more expensive vacations. While it's natural to want to enjoy the rewards of your hard work, continually increasing your lifestyle can prevent you from building long-term wealth.

Misusing Credit Cards

Credit cards can be useful financial tools when used responsibly, but they can also create a false sense of affordability. Many people justify spending because they're earning points, miles, or cash-back rewards. Others repeatedly transfer balances from one card to another, believing they are solving the problem. While promotional offers can provide temporary relief, they don't eliminate the underlying debt. If spending habits don't change, the balance often continues to grow.

Lending Money Out of Guilt

Helping family and friends can feel like the right thing to do, especially when someone you care about is struggling. However, lending money out of guilt, obligation, or fear of disappointing others can put your own financial security at risk. Before helping others, make sure your own financial foundation is stable. Sometimes the most loving response is setting healthy boundaries.

Trying to Buy Love or Ease Guilt

Many parents fall into the trap of spending money to compensate for circumstances they cannot control. Single parents may overspend to make up for an absent parent. Divorced parents may feel pressure to compete with one another through gifts and experiences. Working parents may spend excessively because they feel guilty about the time they cannot spend with their children.

The truth is that children need your presence, guidance, and consistency far more than they need expensive gifts. While it's important to create memories and provide opportunities, using money to ease guilt often creates financial stress without addressing the underlying emotions.

Ignoring the Small Decisions

Financial success is rarely determined by one major decision. It's usually the result of hundreds of small choices made consistently over time. Daily spending habits, recurring subscriptions, impulse purchases, and neglected savings opportunities may seem insignificant individually, but together they can have a significant impact on your financial future.

The Real Lesson

The biggest money mistakes often have little to do with math and everything to do with behavior. When you understand the emotions behind your financial decisions, you gain the power to make choices that support both your current lifestyle and your long-term goals.

Chapter 7
Righting the Ship

If you want to change your financial picture, you must be willing to make changes. In every example that I can share, I will show you a person that had a problem they must solve. They knew that trying to handle it on their own was also not going to make a substantial change. Lastly, they had to be willing to make necessary steps forward to make progress.

So what are you willing to do to change your financial picture? Your financial picture is not limited to your personal finances, but also includes how you want to live. What kind of wealth are you open to build to help you shape the life you want to live for the future.

So what are the steps you need to take to get the improvements you want in life? I have a few suggestions that I recommend to right your ship and change the course of your life. The first step I recommend any one do to get their finances on the right track is to order your credit report.

You need to know what you owe. You need to be clear on what you need to budget for and how you need to clear debts so that you can make real change. As long as you have a laundry list of people you hide from, you will not take ownership of your finances. Hiding will not stop the surprises and threats around the corner that will catch you off guard and at the worse times.

Access Free Resources
Scan or Visit
latoyamaddox.com

To order your report you can use the Book Resource using the QR or visit the website. When pulling your report you will need to get access to all three bureaus. Depending on the purchases you make, one or all three bureaus can receive an inquiry. Any time there is an inquiry into your credit profile it does impact your score, especially for hard inquiries. There are soft pulls, inquiries, that can have little to no impact but you want to limit inquirers until you are in the best position to apply and get approved.

Right now, however, I would try to limit spending. When you are getting your finances on track you don't want to have more money going out unless it will help to achieve your goal of reducing your costs. When most people have to clean up their finances it is not usually because they are not spending enough. More often than not, they are spending too much. When you receive your report you want to look at what you owe and to whom. As you look at your costs and money in and out, you can better your position to make responsible decisions concerning your finances.

Another helpful tip, contest items on your report to see what you can have removed. Contesting charges is how a lot of debt consolidation and credit repair companies work. There are rules to recording debt and these rules are changing quickly. There are new rules emerging from the White House that can benefit many Americans. For example, medical debt was a huge factor that cost many to lose several hundred points because of past due medical bills. With a law like this, those bills will drop off and you can get an unexpected boost!

Other things you can contest and have removed either yourself or with a credit repair company are inquiries, evictions, judgments, charge offs, late payments, and debt greater than 7 years old. In some cases, it is best not to pay the debt but fight to have the debt removed. Making payment arrangements is sometimes necessary but you can negotiate your terms to have the repayment appear more favorable on your credit report.

An easy fix that can help pull your debt inline with your spending budget is to stay home more. I know it sounds simple and even as I saw it some will think, but what am I supposed to do if I cannot hang out and enjoy the money I work hard for? I would suggest finding other things you can do that don't cost as much. Consider how you can spend more time at home because likely your mortgage or rent is the largest bill you pay. We may not think about this, but if you spend so much on where you live, why should it only be the place you eat sometimes and return to just to sleep!

There is more to life and if you want to live life to the fullest, have vacations, date nights, and other activities, you will have to be disciplined to fully enjoy them. A good vacation is not one spent on credit cards where you worry about the repayment later. It is when you are going on vacation and all the expenses are already paid. While you are out having fun, one thing that is not on your mind is, "How will I pay for this?" Having the freedom for this not to be a bullying thought is a relief and helps you to further destress on vacations.

When you look at your home budget I am sure you are seeing some leaky areas. Like, if you have a gym membership that you are not currently using. I personally have a friend who had a gym membership for nearly a year. She went to the gym early on, but then stopped going. Every time she thinks to cancel, she tries to encourage herself to go. In short, she is paying nearly $30 monthly to go to the gym once or not at all. That is a really expensive outing.

This was easily a bill I told her to cut and asked her to consider working out at home, online, using an app, or other method. Turns out she was paying for a yearly subscription for $40 to do workouts at home she was also not using. It is the simple things that we don't pay attention to because they are on subscription. I would encourage you to pay attention to your monthly and annual subscriptions. These seemingly small bills add up over a year. I had this same person cut a $150 monthly bill for a business she wasn't able to pay attention to. She had two entertainment subscriptions she nor her children watched, on top of the gym. She was leaking money on simple things she could easily say no to.

Now, I help my clients look into other monthly bills that might not be as easy to reduce like car payments, rent or mortgage, phone bills, and utilities. We may think that these bills are fixed and will not change, but they also can be reduced. As I have already shared, I help my clients to pull back on their car payments by encouraging them to refinance. You can refinance your house in the same way and shop for lower rates. You can also look at your phone plan and determine if you need all the bells and whistles you have.

An easy fix I notice is with the people who believe they need the latest cell phone or upgrade. If you keep trading your phone in at each turn, you will notice your bill will stay the same if not increase with each upgrade. Try to be patient to get newer devices because as soon as you get it, another will roll out. Keeping up with technology is like keeping up with the Jones's, I don't recommend it. Get what you need and learn to be content with what works.

Being content also means not shopping for every new event. I know for the ladies it can be hard to have a special event or date night and fight the urge not to buy something new. If you take a look at your closet, it is likely already telling you, "No, please don't buy anything else new." If your clothes are oozing out of the closet or your wardrobe has its own bedroom, it is time to cut back on spending in this department. It may also be tempting to buy the latest fashions for your children. I would consider the activity and the quality of clothing you need.

We may look down on second hand stores or places that are non-brand name, but sometimes that is what you need to do to pull your expenses within reach. If you buy something for quality and longevity I can understand that, but that also might mean buying less frequently to keep the expense within budget. I would challenge you to not buy anything new for yourself for at least a year and for your children not more than every 6 months.

This will challenge you to wear things that likely still have a tag on them. Things you never had the chance to wear, you can now pull out, and wear it. So much money is wasted by eating out daily several times per day. When you eat out for every meal, you are spending at least $1,000 a month on food. The quick math, if you spend $15 to $20 per meal, three times per day, that is $60. Multiple that times 30 days, and the total is a whopping $1,800. For those who don't do it every day or even spend $30 per day eating at around $10 per meal, you are still spending $900.

Would you agree that you could afford to eat organic and have snacks all day within half of that budget? People eat at home and bring their lunches to work because they see how much of a financial impact it can have. If you haven't taken the time to look at how much you waste by eating out, I want you to look at your bank or card statement and check. The numbers can startle you.

I know the grocery story is another place where we need to be mindful of spending. Just because we are not spending $900 doesn't mean we should be spending $899. We want to find the right budget for eating what we need and not shopping for what we see that looks good as we walk the isles. It has been proven that stores intentionally place products strategically to get people to buy more. Everything from the music you listen to, to the lighting and smells, all drive your desire to shop.

It is a good habit to go into the store with a listed budget that you try your best to follow. If you need dish soap or something not on the lists, be mindful of how the add ons add to the budget. Buying something just because it is on sale, is not a good enough reason to buy. Stick to what you need and keep focused on your objective to save money. We buy bread, but it might make more financial sense to bake your own brownies, cakes, or sweets. Buying ready made sweets could be the reason your budget is going over.

Having a commitment to stick to your budget can be difficult. For one, you have to discipline yourself. You have to be able to tell yourself no to the things you want. You have to cut back so you can create something for tomorrow. If you spend everything you bring in, you don't have anything for a rainy day that will come. To be successful in budgeting, you have to see that saving today is not robbery against tomorrow. It's about you being responsible about what you have and ensuring there is something for tomorrow.

It may mean starting a side hustle or second job that would allow you to increase your income. When we reach the point where we can save more, we need to look at how we can add more to reach our goals. This could mean getting up earlier, sacrificing time in other places, or cutting back in one place to make room elsewhere. Having more doesn't have to just be in money, it can be in time, skill, or something else. As you sacrifice plans today, don't think that they are not going to positively impact your future. You will make progress and the rewards will be sweet.

At the time, you might not like all the changes you choose to make. Other people may also disagree with your budget rules if it impacts them. If you want to cut back on utilities, you may establish bedtimes, schedule tv time and internet use, or even limit traveling to outside goings for your children as well. It is no secret we spend more when we bring more people. Try grocery shopping when everyone is sleeping or at school. Utility costs are higher in the evening than in the day. Try washing clothes and using the most utilities when the costs are less.

One thing I must mention specifically if you want to change your budget is stop shopping on

Amazon. I know, when I mentioned the other things, you gently said to yourself, "Well, she didn't say I couldn't shop at Amazon." Clicking buttons to order things is an easy way to spend more than anticipated. When you don't see the spending immediately, but the money is taken out when it ships, you may not notice how much you spend on Amazon.

There is a life science called the Amazon effect, which is like reward spending. This is a way we give ourselves for completing tasks we feel no one sees. We can shop on Amazon because we like getting packages in the mail. It is not about if we need it, we just like opening the box and feeling important. Kind of like how some send themselves flowers to feel special, stop it. Stop spending money on Amazon you don't need to and your budget will thank you!

You want to put parameters in place to watch where you waste money, but also, where you waste time. What are you doing with your time? If spending money is the main extra-curricular activity you have, you need to expand your interest. Not everything you do in life should cost you money. If it costs money you don't have, you have to be willing to say no. If you spend a lot of your time surfing the internet, on social apps, watching tv, or something you know isn't adding value, consider changing what you do for some of that time.

Do you know if you spent ten to thirty minutes each day learning something for a year, you could master it in a year to three years? We think to become great we have to slave away for decades; but the truth, you just need to be focused and consistent to see progress. You would be surprised by how your best is not necessary to enter an industry or to earn money. You can work on the level you are currently and make great things happen.

Look at the policies you own and if need be, try to consolidate what you don't need so much of. The enemy to a budget sometimes is not buying what you need or don't need, but buying too much of what you do need. Having too much insurance, too much groceries, too much power/internet, or too much social time. How you balance these functions not only impacts your budget, but also impacts your health.

You want to make sure that in all the things you strive to get out of life, getting or remaining healthy is also high on that list. I recommend having health insurance and even a life insurance policy, preferably whole life if you only have one policy. There are many options you can take for what is a necessity for you, but look at how buying this impacts other things. Too many people have things but no health insurance. To have insurance on a car and not your health doesn't seem wise to me.

If you are willing to cut back now on the things you have been doing, your whole life will thank you.

Bringing your spending in control, your budget will thank you. Enforcing rules for your children to follow will teach them discipline and budgeting. As they get older, they will understand how to pull back on spending when they are off to college or out in the world on their own. Of course, as you pull back on your diet from eating unhealthy foods, cook more at home, and avoid toxic ingredients you will avoid expensive health care later.

Hold My Purse (or Wallet)

When I know I'm heading somewhere that will tempt me to spend, I use a simple strategy: I leave the cards at home and take cash. Before the event, I decide how much I'm willing to spend and that's all I bring. When the cash runs out, the spending stops. No swiping. No "I'll worry about it later." No surprise credit card bill next month. It's a simple way to stay in control, enjoy yourself, and stick to your financial goals without feeling deprived.

Remember as you right your ship, you are not just becoming a penny pincher, cheap, frugal, or a tightwad. You are shaping your future with the decisions you are making today. If you need help to right your ship and get things in order, or to have accountability, I share with you my Wealth Builder course, an invaluable resource that has helped individuals and families to realign their finances.

If you are serious about changing your financial picture, you have to become focused on wealth building and not spending all you have and living paycheck to paycheck. You have to decide that this kind of life is one you don't want and I can help you turn the ship around. So if you need me, start here with this course if you don't call me for additional support.

Access Free Resources
Scan or Visit
latoyamaddox.com

Chapter 8
Staying the Course

I believe now you are starting to see the benefits of what a financial planner can do for you. Yes, we look at your finances and we help people with everyday problems. Sometimes we may feel like where we are starting, we don't have enough to hire or work with a financial planner. I pray that theory has also been proven to be false.

Everyone can learn to be better with money. We all can learn how to save, yes, but most of us need to learn how to invest. There are more ways to invest than betting on the stock market. There are other options that are more secure and offer more ideal returns. A goal of your financial planner is to show you how to save more and make what you have stretch farther.

We don't know what we don't know. So if you will allow me to show you how you can close the gap on ensuring the hard work you have done thus far. Let me show you how your future can have some security. Yes, we don't control the outcomes of GDP and inclusive economics, but there is a way to ensure you have some kind of retirement if you properly plan for it using multiple vehicles.

Take for example my client Jennifer. She was 50 years old at the time when she walked into my office. Her desire was to relocate to Florida and enjoy the sun and her retirement. There are many differences between the city in which she lived and the rules for the state she planned to move to. One, she had property that she had to make decisions about. Two, she had to understand how the tax code and laws in Florida varied from where she currently lived.

My assignment was to help her make the best financial decisions in this situation. I helped her understand the tax laws in Florida so she could make the best decision when selling her property. I adjusted her estate plan to reflect Florida's laws. I also recommended a mix of municipal bonds and real estate income trusts (REITs) to preserve cash flow.

What I love is I helped her to liquidate her assets to purchase a home in cash from the money she sat aside from the sale. I showed her how to manage her money so it would last as long as her retirement. What I really gave Jennifer is peace of mind.

She is now able to enjoy the sun and the house that she bought without issue. I think more of us would like to do the same thing, and if you want to do this, I can point you to the road that makes the most sense for you. A good planner begins with your goals and determines how to get you there with what you have to start with.

Take for example Rachel, a single mother 40 years old. She was employed as a mid-level HR manager. She made a decent income, and she appeared to be in good health and happy. But looking more into her finances, she was not set up how she needed to be to provide for her children or protect herself.

She had no will or guardianship plan for her children. The minimal life insurance coverage she received from work she didn't have an updated beneficiary. For the house she was buying, she had no plan for how to pass down the asset with available safeguards.

In this case, I had to partner with an estate attorney to draft a will, naming guardians for her children and establishing a trust to manage funds for their care and education. I helped Rachel increase her coverage to $750,000 to ensure financial security for her children if something happened to her. I also updated her beneficiaries to reflect her children's trust.

We didn't stop there, I also updated her retirement accounts and savings to ensure they were aligned with her estate plan. Creating an emergency fund was also high on the list, and I encouraged Rachel to create a "legacy binder" with important documents and passwords to simplify things for her children's guardian.

Rachel gained a peace of mind knowing her children's future was secure and that her assets would be distributed according to her wishes. The best benefit of having a plan is that you know what to do in times of emergency. The other bonus, you know what to do in times of a surplus and when things are going great.

I will encourage anyone to set up a viable business to earn additional income. If your income is not where it needs to be to help you achieve your goals quickly, adding a business can be the way to get there. However, starting a business and weaving it into your financial plan might not be easy to do–even if you have the money for many of us.

One thing I love to do is to help enthusiastic entrepreneurs to set up their businesses and life for success. You shouldn't have to choose between making money and investing. They both should go together, and my fast track for business owners to align the two has helped many navigate launching their business and working it into their financial future.

Get Estate Planning help or launch your business with Quantum Leap. Scan the QR or visit the resource page to get started.

Access Free Resources
Scan or Visit
latoyamaddox.com

To get from where you are to where you want to be, saving, although impactful, is not the way to go solely. You cannot save your way to financial freedom but must take a leap into the investing or business world. The industry doesn't matter because all businesses have a similar pattern. I created a program I call Quantum Leap Your Business, because it is a leap of faith to do something you are not sure will work.

Be open to learn and grow when you start your business. Things can change quickly, so in my course that is 6 weeks long, I show new business owners what to expect and how to navigate changes. Starting a business doesn't have to be scary or intimidating if you know what to do.

Yes, some answers will be right out front, and others, you will have to learn and grow through. In this program I start with "Creation and Clarity." Before you can sell a thing, you have to be clear on what you intend to do and how you expect to help others. Business is all about being a tool, and offering a skill that can impact other people's lives for the better.

All businesses have to establish some key connections to know where to find money, supplies, and their ideal clients. I speak about networking and how to build relationships that last and will help to build your business in the "Connections" module. After connections, we move on to "Communication." How you speak to people and what you talk about is important.

You want to establish your brand and business as a trustworthy and accredited option for clients. To do this, you want to ensure your communication is solid. You have to take the time to think through your messaging, mission and vision statements, and get everything flowing in the same direction. This module is set on helping business owners accomplish this with useful tools.

"Capitalization" is the plan you want to have for how you will make money. This module is important. A business without a plan to make money is a dream. I want to show you how to bring your dreams into you reality. This takes planning and thought. This module is dedicated to the tough questions and helping you determine how to move your vision ahead.

Making money is great, but keeping and growing it is better. To advance your business you will need good referrals. Compliments and recommendations come from being consistent, committed to quality services, and setting goals for yourself and the clients. When you set benchmarks and meet or exceed them, your ideal client will take note and respond. "Commitment and Goal Setting" is a step that might be easy to pass up, but don't.

Knowing your goals and being committed to reach them will help you establish your business. Opening a business can be tough and challenging. In module six, I deal with how to set the right culture within yourself and your office to keep everyone motivated. "Cultivation and Motivation" are paired together because you cannot have one without the other. You have to set the tone for your organization even if you are starting off as a member of one. Your attitude represents how everyone else will approach your business.

Staying motivated is a must for the hard times up ahead. There will be challenges and remembering why you started the business is important. The key to staying motivated is knowing why you got started in the first place and keeping your eyes on who you intended to help.

Another aspect to starting a business or anything in life, is you have to believe in yourself. You have to have a positive mindset, and I will say a winning mindset about what you set out to do. If you are negative about your future, and that's what you see and speak, your words can shape the outcomes of your future. As a bonus, I give you tools and tips for how to keep a winning mindset and eliminate limiting beliefs.

When you tap into your gifts and remember what makes you special and powerful, it will fuel your future. I believe those who have an entrepreneurial spirit have an untapped gift that must be shared. Not only for your financial breakthrough, but also to fulfill your purpose. Helping business owners is my passion because I have been there too. I wanted to have someone to help me through those tough times in the very beginning, and now I offer that to business owners.

I am all about being a solution and a help to people. If you pull anything away from my book, I want you to remember that I am just like you. I am a woman with dreams, ambitions, who had to learn how to navigate making my business work amongst getting educated and having the knowledge to get it done. The best part, now that I have the knowledge I am empowered to help others do the same with less of a learning curve.

No one can pick your path forward but you, but a good advisor will give you options so you don't feel stuck or hopeless. You can change your future and I prove that it is possible with my own life story. I have been married, divorced, a single mother, and married again. Life has twists and turns, but money doesn't have to be a huge pendulum swing. There is a way to stabilize your life and bring peace to your mind.

We do the best work when we are at ease, and it is my passion to help you do that. If I can be of help, please use the QRs in this book to contact me and take advantage of my free tools. If you would like to contact me with questions or for a free evaluation, please use the QR below.

Access Free Resources

Scan or Visit

latoyamaddox.com

Lastly, to thank you for completing this book, I have a special gift for you! When we do something good I am a firm believer in rewards. Positive reinforcement can go a long way, and if you haven't been doing this, start today. Start complimenting yourself for what you accomplish. If you have a running list of things to do, when you complete one of them, give yourself a pat on the back somehow.

This doesn't mean going out and spending money, but it could mean taking a candle light bath. Playing music, watching some TV, or scrolling on social apps. Finding things to do to help you relax is important and I want to share with you some tools that I think you can use while you are relaxed and not worried about the numbers.

If you like the gift, I ask you to connect with me on social media and tell me about your experience. Until our meeting, it has been a pleasure.

"What is the one financial habit you could improve this month that would have the biggest impact on your future?"

~ LaToya

About the Author

LaToya Maddox

LaToya Maddox, MBA, CPRM ™, CES®, CFP®, is a financial planner, investment advisor, and founder of Infinity Financial Wealth Management, LLC, a boutique financial planning firm serving high-achieving women and families who want clarity, confidence, and control over their financial future.

With over 25 years of experience in financial services, LaToya specializes in retirement income planning, tax-aware investing, risk management, and legacy planning. She is passionate about helping women — especially those navigating transition such as divorce, widowhood, or career reinvention — move from financial uncertainty to financial security.

Known for her practical wisdom and empowering approach, LaToya believes that financial security begins in the mind. Her work focuses not just on numbers, but on behavior, discipline, and decision-making — because lasting wealth is built from the inside out.

In addition to leading her firm, LaToya is a member of Zeta Phi Beta Sorority, Incorporated. She contributes to programs focused on community impact, service, and economic advancement —values that directly inform her work in building generational wealth and financial confidence.

LaToya lives in Georgia with her husband, Donald, and their children, Joseph, Joshua, and Logan. When she's not helping clients build financial clarity, she enjoys traveling, running, reading, and mentoring the next generation of leaders.

Change Your Mind, Change Your Money is her call to action for anyone ready to take ownership of their financial future and build security that lasts.

About *the Author*

Explore and learn more about published authors affiliated with KLE.

KLEPub.com

www.ingramcontent.com/pod-product-compliance
Lightning Source LLC
LaVergne TN
LVHW022101200926
848481LV00003B/1021
* 9 7 9 8 8 9 9 8 7 9 4 5 6 *